Zhoutun

This book presents a description of the grammar of Zhoutun, an endangered Sinitic variety spoken by fewer than 1,000 people in the Qinghai Province of northwest China. With vocabulary predominantly from Chinese and Tibetan syntax, Zhoutun is one of the Sinitic varieties most distant from Mandarin Chinese, with unexpected typological features like, for example, case markers, rigid SOV word order, simplified tonal system, negative copula as a disjunctive coordinator and a "locutor-referential pronoun" which is not found in Chinese and in many other languages.

Zhoutun is also a representative variety of the Gansu-Qinghai linguistic area in which Mongolic and Turkic languages coexist with Tibetan and Chinese dialects from a long time ago. This book also describes the sociolinguistic and sociohistorical contexts of Zhoutun.

It should be of interest to specialists and students of language contact, linguistic typology, Chinese dialectology, language geography, anthropological linguistics, sociolinguistics, folklore studies and preservation of endangered languages.

Chenlei Zhou is an associate professor at the Institute of Linguistics, Chinese Academy of Social Sciences. His main research interests are linguistic typology, language contact and Chinese grammar, and he has published more than 20 articles in journals such as *Lingua*; *Language and Linguistics*; and the *Journal of Chinese Linguistics*.

Routledge World Languages

Routledge World Languages provides modern and up-to-date basic grammatical descriptions of understudied languages around the world, with particular attention to the minority, the endangered, and the extinct languages. Each volume contains a grammar sketch describing particular aspects of the structure (phonology, morphology, and syntax) of a single language as well as sociolinguistic and historical information to complement the overview of that language.

The volumes of the *Routledge World Languages* are intended for a broad audience, including students and scholars of Documentary and Descriptive Linguistics, Linguistics Typology, Endangered Languages, and Anthropology, community languages teachers, and the general public. The series aims to give the reader an understanding of the diversity of historical-natural languages in general.

South Picene
Raoul Zamponi

Tondano
A Grammar Sketch of an Endangered Minahasan Language
Timothy Brickell

Zhoutun
Chenlei Zhou

For more information about this series, please visit: www.routledge.com/Routledge-World-Languages/book-series/RWL

Zhoutun

Chenlei Zhou

LONDON AND NEW YORK

First published 2022
by Routledge
4 Park Square, Milton Park, Abingdon, Oxon OX14 4RN

and by Routledge
605 Third Avenue, New York, NY 10158

Routledge is an imprint of the Taylor & Francis Group, an informa business

© 2022 Chenlei Zhou

The right of Chenlei Zhou to be identified as author of this work has been asserted in accordance with sections 77 and 78 of the Copyright, Designs and Patents Act 1988.

All rights reserved. No part of this book may be reprinted or reproduced or utilised in any form or by any electronic, mechanical, or other means, now known or hereafter invented, including photocopying and recording, or in any information storage or retrieval system, without permission in writing from the publishers.

Trademark notice: Product or corporate names may be trademarks or registered trademarks, and are used only for identification and explanation without intent to infringe.

British Library Cataloguing-in-Publication Data
A catalogue record for this book is available from the British Library

Library of Congress Cataloging-in-Publication Data
A catalog record has been requested for this book

ISBN: 978-1-032-11317-3 (hbk)
ISBN: 978-1-032-11318-0 (pbk)
ISBN: 978-1-003-21936-1 (ebk)

DOI: 10.4324/9781003219361

Typeset in Times New Roman
by Apex CoVantage, LLC

To my wife 张文萱.

Contents

Preface   xii

1 Introduction   1
  1.1 Genetic affiliation 1
  1.2 Typological profile 2
  1.3 Sociolinguistic, sociohistorical and areal context 3
    1.3.1 Sociolinguistic context 3
    1.3.2 Sociohistorical context 4
    1.3.3 Areal context 4
    1.3.4 Theory and data 5

2 Phonology   7
  2.1 Consonants 7
    2.1.1 Stops 7
    2.1.2 Fricatives 8
    2.1.3 Affricates 8
    2.1.4 Nasals 8
    2.1.5 Lateral 8
    2.1.6 Approximate 8
  2.2 Vowels 9
    2.2.1 Basic vowels 9
    2.2.2 Nasal vowels 9
    2.2.3 Vowel sequences 10
  2.3 Word tones 10
  2.4 R-ization and reduplication 12
    2.4.1 r-ization 12
    2.4.2 Reduplication 13
  2.5 Syllable structure 13

3 Nouns and noun phrases — 14
3.1 Definition 14
3.2 Word formation 15
   3.2.1 Affixation 15
   3.2.2 Reduplication 17
   3.2.3 Compounding 18
3.3 Number 19
   3.3.1 =mɤ 19
   3.3.2 =liɛ 21
3.4 Case relations 22
   3.4.1 Dative-accusative =xa/=a 22
   3.4.2 Comitative-instrumental =lã 24
   3.4.3 Ablative =tha 26
   3.4.4 Locative =li and =xã 26
   3.4.5 Genitive =tɤ 28
   3.4.6 Comparative khã 28
3.5 Referentiality 29
   3.5.1 Generic 29
   3.5.2 Individual 30

4 Verbs and verb phrases — 32
4.1 Definition 32
4.2 Aspect 33
   4.2.1 Perfective 33
   4.2.2 Future 34
   4.2.3 Ingressive 35
   4.2.4 Progressive 36
   4.2.5 Resultative 37
   4.2.6 Experiential 38
   4.2.7 The expression of tense 38
4.3 Modality 39
   4.3.1 Dynamic modality 39
   4.3.2 Epistemic modality 41
   4.3.3 Deontic modality 42
   4.3.4 Evidentiality 44
   4.3.5 Negation 45
4.4 Serial verb constructions 46

4.5 *Verb-complement constructions 49*
    4.5.1 Verb-direction constructions 49
    4.5.2 Verb-result constructions 52
    4.5.3 Verb-degree constructions 52
4.6 *Valence changing 53*
4.7 *Possession and existence 58*

5 Adjectives and adverbs   59
5.1 *Adjectives 59*
    5.1.1 Identify adjectives and verbs 59
    5.1.2 Adjectives as modifiers 62
    5.1.3 Adjectives as predicates 63
5.2 *Adverbs 64*
    5.2.1 Position 64
    5.2.2 Some common adverbs 66
    5.2.3 Reduplication 68

6 Minor word classes   69
6.1 *Pronoun 69*
    6.1.1 First person 69
    6.1.2 Second person 70
    6.1.3 Third person 70
    6.1.4 Reflexive 71
    6.1.5 Locutor-referential 71
6.2 *Demonstratives 77*
    6.2.1 The system 77
    6.2.2 Animate and inanimate referents 77
    6.2.3 Location referents 79
    6.2.4 Manner and degree 81
6.3 *Interrogative words 81*
    6.3.1 tuɤ- words 81
    6.3.2 a- words 82
    6.3.3 -mɤ words 83
    6.3.4 Others 84
6.4 *Numerals 86*
    6.4.1 Cardinal and ordinal numerals 86
    6.4.2 Fractional numerals 86

6.5 Classifiers 87
   6.5.1 Nominal classifiers 87
   6.5.2 Verbal classifiers 88
   6.5.3 The position of Num+CL and noun 88
6.6 Final particles 90
   6.6.1 ti 90
   6.6.2 pa 92
   6.6.3 li 93
   6.6.4 xuã 95
   6.6.5 kɤ 96
   6.6.6 ta 98
   6.6.7 ia 99
   6.6.8 mɤ 100
   6.6.9 pɨ 101
   6.6.10 sa 102
   6.6.11 Summary 104
6.7 Adpositions 105
   6.7.1 Prepositions 105
   6.7.2 Postpositions 107
6.8 Coordinators 108
   6.8.1 Conjunctive coordinator 109
   6.8.2 Disjunctive coordinators 110

7 Clause structure   116
7.1 Word order 116
7.2 Ditransitive construction 118
7.3 Copula clause 119
7.4 Comparative clause 122
   7.4.1 Comparative construction 122
   7.4.2 Comparative construction of equality 126
   7.4.3 Superlative construction 126
7.5 Imperative clause 126
   7.5.1 The form of imperative clauses 126
   7.5.2 The negation of imperative clauses 130
7.6 Interrogative clause 131
   7.6.1 Yes-no questions 131
   7.6.2 Wh- questions 131
   7.6.3 Alternative question 132
   7.6.4 Tag question 132

7.7 Subordinate clause 134
  7.7.1 Relative clause 134
  7.7.2 Complement clause 135
  7.7.3 Adverbial clause 136
7.8 Topic structure 137

References	139
Appendices	143
I. Text "The past life in Zhoutun" 143	
II. List of abbreviations 157	
Index	159

Preface

This book is a grammar of Zhoutun, a Chinese variety spoken in Guide County, Qinghai Province, and hugely influenced by Amdo Tibetan. This book is divided into seven parts. Chapter 1 is an introduction. Chapter 2 discusses the phonology. Chapter 3 deals with nouns and noun phrases, in which word formation, number, case relations and referentiality are discussed. Chapter 4 is concerned with verbs and verb phrases. Aspect, modality, serial verb constructions, verb-complement constructions, valence changing, possession and existence are involved in this chapter. Chapter 5 discusses adjectives and adverbs. The minor word classes, including pronouns, demonstratives, interrogative words, numerals, classifiers, final particles, adpositions and coordinators, are introduced in Chapter 6. Chapter 7 concerns clause structure, in which word order, ditransitive constructions, copula clauses, comparative clauses, imperative clauses, interrogative clauses, subordinate clauses and topic structure are discussed.

Due to the language contact, Zhoutun represents an extreme Sinitic variety that exhibits a number of typological characteristics that are different from those of Mandarin Chinese. It has Chinese vocabulary and Tibetan syntax, and at the same time, on the syntactic level alone, it also shows a transition between the Tibetan type and the Chinese type in many respects.

The data used in this book are derived from my four-time fieldwork during the period 2014–20. Since September 2014, I have conducted field research at the village of Zhoutun and collected a great deal of firsthand data. In 2016, I successfully defended my doctoral dissertation entitled *Qinghai Zhoutunhua Cankao Yufa* [A Reference Grammar of Zhoutun in Qinghai Province]. Since then, I have continuously concentrated on Zhoutun and the Gan-Qing linguistic area and gained a deeper understanding of many phenomena detailed in this book.

Hopefully, this book has been helpful in documenting the basic grammatical aspects of this endangered Sinitic variety, which is spoken by only 800–900 people, and in providing a living example for the study of the

Sino-Tibetan family and language contact (especially in the Gan-Qing linguistic area).

I would like to express my special gratitude to the series editor, Raoul Zamponi, who read it carefully and made numerous comments and revisions that ensured the quality of the publication. Thanks to the anonymous reviewers, who made valuable and inspiring comments. I am also thankful to Andrea Hartill, Ellie Auton, Iola Ashby, Questina Teo and Kate Fornadel at Routledge. Without their work, this book would not have been published. Of course, any remaining errors are mine.

I would also like to take this opportunity to express my gratitude to Dan Xu, Kai Sun, Keith Slater, Donald Winford, as well as many other experts and friends. They have helped me in various ways in the study of Zhoutun, the Gan-Qing linguistic area and language contact.

My thanks also go to the Chinese National Social Science Foundation "Corpus of grammatical features of Chinese Dialects" (19AYY004) and European Research Council (ERC)–funded research project "Tracing language and population mixing in the Gansu-Qinghai area", ERC-2019-AdG, 883700-TRAM.

1 Introduction

1.1 Genetic affiliation

Zhoutun (周屯话 *Zhoutunhua* in Chinese) is a northwest Chinese (Mandarin) variety spoken by about 800–900 people in Zhoutun Village, Guide County, Hainan Tibetan Autonomous Prefecture, Qinghai Province, P.R. China. Unlike other northwest Chinese varieties, Zhoutun was deeply influenced by Amdo Tibetan, and its basic word order was changed to a rigid SOV. In harmony with the SOV order, Zhoutun has a set of postpositions and postpositional case markers that do not exist or rarely exist in Mandarin Chinese with an SVO order.

Although the syntactic profile of Zhoutun has a number of features that can be classified into the Tibetan type, Zhoutun is basically a northwest Chinese variety, rather than a Tibetan one. This is because the basic vocabulary and grammatical morphemes of Zhoutun are from Chinese and have clear cognate forms in Mandarin Chinese. The question of whether Zhoutun should be classified as a Chinese dialect, a distinct Sinitic language or a mixed language is, however, still an open question, which largely depends on the criteria one would adopt to define a language or a dialect. In a study on Wutun, a Sinitic variety spoken, like Zhoutun, in Qinghai Province and, like Zhoutun, under the huge influence of nearby non-Sinitic languages (mainly Amdo Tibetan), Sandman (2016, 2) argues that since it is unintelligible to the speakers who speak other Mandarin Chinese dialects, she has defined Wutun as a "distinct Sinitic language" rather than a Chinese dialect. While it makes sense to consider intelligibility, the question is whether intelligibility is the sole factor to take into account in classifying a language variety. In Chinese literature, a number of "unintelligible" varieties, such as Wu, Min, and Cantonese, are defined as Chinese dialects instead of distinct languages. The same is true for "mixed languages" like Zhoutun: scholars have different criteria to define a mixed language. Wutun, for example, is considered by different authors as a Sinitic language (Sandman 2016), a mixed language (Li 1983; Slater 2003) or a variety of Chinese (Thomason and Kaufman 1988; Janhunen et al. 2008). Regardless of which specific

DOI: 10.4324/9781003219361-1

linguistic identity Zhoutun is defined as, I believe the objective description of the Zhoutun grammar will not be affected by the terminological issue. And in this book, I would conveniently use "Zhoutun" to indicate the language spoken in the village of Zhoutun.

1.2 Typological profile

A striking phonological peculiarity of Zhoutun in the Sinitic context lies in its tonal system. Zhoutun has only two phonemic tones: the low-rise '13' and the high '55'. As two-tone systems are atypical in Sinitic, one can either assert that in Zhoutun there are two tones or argue for a distinction between low vs. high or non-stressed vs. stressed (as in the analysis of Sandman 2016 for Wutun[1]). In this book, I argue that lexical tones rather than phonemic tones play a significant role in the tonal system of Zhoutun.

Unlike Mandarin Chinese, which is generally considered an analytic and isolating language, Zhoutun has a hybrid analytic-agglutinative system, in which more clitics (or even affixes) such as postpositions and aspect markers are found than in Mandarin Chinese. The basic word order of Zhoutun is SOV, as indicated previously. Note that this verb-final pattern is rigid: being definite or indefinite, the object always precedes the verb. In contrast, in some northwest Chinese varieties with mixed features which are spoken in the same area (such as Tangwang and Xining), while a definite object precedes the verb, an indefinite object is placed after the verb, coherently with the preferred SOV order. As far as ditransitive constructions are concerned, their basic word order in Zhoutun is ARTV, where A is the agent, R the recipient-like role, T the theme-like role and V is the verb: a word order in line with the OV pattern.

At the subclausal level (such as NP, VP, etc.), Zhoutun represents typical features of OV languages, i.e., it has a significant number of correlation pairs (Dryer 1992) with OV:

(1) OV correlation pairs found in Zhoutun
    a NP-adposition;
    b Predicative-copula verb;
    c VP-tense/aspect auxiliary verb;
    d Genitive-noun;
    e Comparative standard-adjective;
    f Prepositional phrase-verb;
    g Manner adverb-verb.

See Section 7.1 for details on the word order.

1.3 Sociolinguistic, sociohistorical and areal context

1.3.1 Sociolinguistic context

Zhoutun village has 882 settlers, of which 85 percent are Han, 10 percent are Tibetans, and 5 percent are Monguor/Tu.[2] All the Han, whose population numbers approximately 750, fluently use Zhoutun in daily conversation. Because of the lack of specific investigation, the current level of bilingualism for the Tibetans and Monguor/Tu people in the village is unclear. According to my general observation, when communicating with the Han people in the village, the Monguor/Tu people tend to use Zhoutun, while Tibetans use Tibetan. Since my data were only collected from the Han people, the grammar system described in this book is actually restricted to the Zhoutun spoken by local Han residents.

The Han people in the village, particularly those older than 80 years, can speak Amdo Tibetan as well. Unfortunately, since they are few in number and have poor health (they rarely go out to meet Tibetans), I was unable to obtain data from their conversations with Tibetans. Nonetheless, one of my instructors, Qiulan Xu (born in 1933), assured me that when she was young, the Han people in the Zhoutun village frequently communicated with the nearby Tibetans in Amdo Tibetan. Currently, a certain number of middle-aged speakers (close to 40 years old) can speak Amdo Tibetan, particularly merchants who often conduct business with Tibetans in nearby villages.

The younger generation, however, has a lower level of fluency in Amdo Tibetan. They are more familiar with the Mandarin variety called Qiaohua (a local variety of the Xining dialect spoken in Guide County, 22 kilometers from the Zhoutun village) for two main reasons. First, with social development, a villager finds moving to a developed county more convenient and is more eager to do so. Second, as part of the compulsory education, teenagers of the Zhoutun village are sent to boarding schools in the county, where their classmates come from the county and other villages and Qiaohua is used as a common language. In fact, due to this expanded communication with people outside the village, many elder people in the Zhoutun village master Qiaohua, too.

Another language that influences Zhoutun is Mandarin Chinese, whose penetration occurs mainly through TV programs.[3] Its influence, however, is more minor than that of Qiaohua, and people differ in whether they can or want to use Mandarin Chinese to converse with outsiders (such as me). Moreover, their "Mandarin Chinese" greatly interferes with Zhoutun in, e.g., tones and word order.

1.3.2 Sociohistorical context

Based on Zhe (2001), the history of the Zhoutun village can be traced back to the Ming dynasty (1368–1644 AD). In 1406, the Ming government dispatched troops to defend Guide County from the surrounding Tibetans, and these people came from Hezhou, currently Linxia, Gansu Province. The ancestors of the current residents of Zhoutun then settled down and built the village under the leadership of Officer 周鉴 Jian Zhou. It is after him the Zhoutun was named: *Zhoutun* literally means "Zhou's camp". Zhoutun was then built mainly to resist the nearby Tibetans. In fact, the geographical proximity of Zhoutun and the surrounding Tibetan villages continues to this day: Zhoutun village is now surrounded by 11 Tibetan villages. During its long-term contact with these neighbor communities, Zhoutun has been influenced in many respects by Tibetans in terms of culture and language.

A number of villagers in Zhoutun practice Tibetan Buddhism. Currently, two religious places of worship can be found in Zhoutun: the Erlang Temple 二郎庙 and the Zhoutun Temple 周屯寺. Among them, the Erlang Temple is dedicated to the god Erlang, who is proper of the Chinese culture but was brought by Tibetan monks and recognized by Tibetans.[4] The temple is opened for worship on the 1st, 8th and 15th days of each lunar month, and Tibetans are also seen visiting. During the worship, some rituals are not inherent to Chinese culture, but there are clear manifestations of Tibetan Buddhism, such as simmering sang "pine and cypress branches". Although the Zhoutun Temple has been closed for many years, it was a place of worship for the villagers of Zhoutun in the early days. In addition, Tibetan elements in medical therapy, food (such as ghee), clothing (sheepskin jacket and clothes worn on specific festivals), burial (sky burial), legends (such as "Cat Ghosts and Gods"), etc. were or still are affecting the material and spiritual life of the Zhoutun villagers.

1.3.3 Areal context

Zhoutun is not the only mixed Sinitic variety that has been shaped by the influence of non-Sinitic languages in the surrounding area. In fact, Zhoutun is located in a region where a deep language contact occurs: the Gan-Qing linguistic area (also referred to as "Qinghai-Gansu Sprachbund" and "Amdo Sprachbund" in literature, such as in Slater 2003 and Sandman 2016, respectively). In this region, we find a number of Sinitic varieties (such as Tangwang, Gan'gou, etc.), Amdo Tibetan, Mongolic languages (Santa, Bonan, Mongghul) and Turkic languages (such as Western Yugur and Salar), which have been in contact with each other for a long time and have developed some regional characteristics, such as the use of the comitative-instrumental marker originated from the element meaning "two" shared by the Sinitic varieties and the Mongolic and Turkic languages of the area (cf. Zhou 2022).

Language contact has led to more or less deep changes in all the languages and dialects of the Gan-Qing linguistic area. The most affected varieties are the Sinitic ones, which have undergone the significant shift from VO to OV in syntax. Xu (2014) points out that the Sinitic varieties in this area share a series of atypical features: (i) a basic OV, rather than VO, word order; (ii) a system of enclitic case markers; (iii) plural markers that can be attached to inanimate nouns; (iv) a morpheme *zhe* used between two VPs in order to link the VPs; (v) the occurrence of the verb "say" after its object clause; and (vi) a simplification of the tonal system.

By examining case markers in the Gan-Qing linguistic area, I argued that there are two major strata of contact within the region: the earlier contact between Sinitic varieties and Amdo Tibetan and the later contact with Mongolic languages (Zhou 2020a). Through the most recent fieldwork in October 2020, I noticed that, at least in Zhoutun, Mandarin Chinese is increasingly influential in the local speech. A similar situation is found in Tangwang (Xu and Ran 2020), indicating that language contact is still ongoing and deserves attention.

1.3.4 Theory and data

This book examines the grammatical system of Zhoutun by utilizing the framework and findings of contemporary linguistic typology, and, in particular, of Dixon's basic linguistic theory (Dixon 2010) and Aikhenvald's (2015) framework. The basic linguistic theory is a "frame-neutral" theory which permits describing a language without presupposing a theoretical framework. Aikhenvald (2015) shows in detail how various grammatical categories are cross-linguistically represented and provides a good reference for my investigation and descriptions. In addition, I also make use of the linguistic inventory typology (LIT) developed by Liu (2011). Rather than a predetermined specific framework in language description, LIT is a theoretical perspective that focuses on the two-way interaction between form and meaning in languages. Through this perspective, it is possible to take good note of how a form that mainly belongs to one category is also used in other categories (e.g., the directional verb *lɛ* 'come' in Zhoutun also conveys a modal meaning) and how a particular semantic category is expressed by multiple forms (e.g., certain aspectual meanings in Zhoutun can be expressed either by aspect markers attached to the verb or by the particle *li*). All this helped me to portray the grammatical system of Zhoutun in a, hopefully, accessible way.

The data in this book were collected during my four times of fieldwork in the village of Zhoutun in September to October 2014, November 2014 to

January 2015, August to September 2015, and in October 2020, for a total of nearly five months. The data were collected from two sources: structured interviews and natural discourse, which, in turn, includes interviews on specific topics, storytelling and daily conversations. Since the data of natural discourse does not permit distinguishing with certainty what is grammatical and ungrammatical and many uncommon (but grammatical) constructions are hard to observe in natural discourse, I preferred to mainly utilize structured interviews. I tried to avoid using Mandarin Chinese during data collection, but in the beginning of the investigation, as I did not understand Zhoutun, I used Mandarin Chinese to try to communicate with some younger villagers.

I did not use the sentences that are collected simply by asking the native speakers to translate a Mandarin sentence into Zhoutun. A common situation was like this: (i) I asked a collaborator "How to say 'I ate three apples' in Zhoutun?" and I could get an answer such as "I apple=*xa* three ate"; (ii) then, in daily conversation, if I found the exact sentence "I apple=*xa* three ate", I could judge that this was a native expression; or (iii) when I became familiar with Zhoutun, I would construct a sentence "I apple=*xa* three ate" and ask an informant whether it was a native expression. If it was, I replaced its constituents and constructed other sentences, such as "He banana=*xa* two ate" or "Zhaxi food=*xa* one ate" to further examine their acceptability. If the result was an ungrammatical construction, I replaced the constituents and formed other sentences for further judgment, asking the informant to correct the sentence.

In total, nearly 1,400 sentences were collected through this type of interview. Seventeen stories, interviews and daily conversations were also recorded and transcribed (but not in a strict IPA phonetic transcription). The material I gathered includes over 25,000 words.

Notes

1 Interestingly, some scholars who have worked on Wutun do claim that it has no phonemic tones. Li (1983), for example, states that Wutun "has entirely lost phonemic tones". Acuo & Xiang (2015), however, argue that Wutun has two tones. This situation is analogous to that of Zhoutun. I believe that whether Wutun and Zhoutun have a phonemic tone system is a matter of analysis rather than a linguistic (phonetic) fact.
2 These demographic data are based on the official statistics in 2014.
3 With Mandarin Chinese I refer to Putonghua 普通话, i.e., Modern Standard Chinese.
4 For a foreign religious icon to be worshiped by Tibetans, it needs to be first introduced by an authoritative Tibetan Buddhist leader and then recognized by the Tibetan people.

2 Phonology

2.1 Consonants

The consonant inventory of Zhoutun is shown in Table 2.1.

Table 2.1 Consonant phonemes

	Bilabial	Labio-dental	Alveolar	Retroflex	Alveolo-palatal	Velar
Stops	p pʰ		t tʰ			k kʰ
Fricative		f	s	ʂ	ɕ	x
Affricate			ts tsʰ	tʂ tʂʰ	tɕ tɕʰ	
Nasal	m		n			ŋ
Lateral			l			
Approximate				ɻ		

2.1.1 Stops

Zhoutun has three pairs of stops that contrast with regard to aspiration.

(1) /p/ vs. /pʰ/
    a [pa] 八 'eight'
    b [pʰa] 怕 'afraid'

(2) /t/ vs. /tʰ/
    a [ta] 打 'beat'
    b [tʰa] 塔 'towel'

(3) /k/ vs. /kʰ/
    a [ka] 尕 'small'
    b [kʰã] 看 'look'

DOI: 10.4324/9781003219361-2

2.1.2 Fricatives

There are five fricatives in Zhoutun, differing in the place of articulation.

(4)   a   Labio-dental /f/: [fɑ̃] 房 'house'
      b   Alveolar /s/: [si] 死 'death'
      c   Retroflex /ʂ/: [ʂɯ] 手 'hand'
      d   Alveolo-palatal /ɕ/: [ɕia] 下 'down'
      e   Velar /x/: [xɔ] 好 'good'

2.1.3 Affricates

Three pairs of affricates, contrasting with regard to aspiration, occur in Zhoutun.

(5)   /ts/ vs. /tsʰ/
      a   [tsi] 字 'character'
      b   [tsʰi] 词 'word'

(6)   /tʂ/ vs. /tʂʰ/
      a   [tʂi] 知 'know'
      b   [tʂʰi] 吃 'eat'

(7)   /tɕ/ vs. /tɕʰ/
      a   [tɕi] 鸡 'chicken'
      b   [tɕʰi] 去 'go'

2.1.4 Nasals

There are three nasals in Zhoutun.

(8)   a   /m/: [ma] 妈 'mother'
      b   /n/: [na] 拿 'take'
      c   /ŋ/: [ŋɤ] 我 'I'

2.1.5 Lateral

The lateral consonant in Zhoutun is /l/, as in [lɛ] 来 'come'.

2.1.6 Approximate

The approximate consonant in Zhoutun is /ɻ/, as in [ɻɤ] 热 'hot'.

2.2 Vowels

2.2.1 Basic vowels

Zhoutun has the nine basic vowels given in Table 2.2.

Table 2.2 Basic vowels

	Front		Central	Back	
Close	i	y	ɨ	ɯ	u
Close-mid				ɤ	
Open-mid	ɛ				ɔ
Open	a				

The vowel /i/ has three allophones, namely, [i], [ɿ] and [ʅ]. Of the three, [ɿ] occurs when /i/ follows /s/, /ts/ or /tsʰ/; while [ʅ] follows /ʂ/, /tʂ/ or /tʂʰ/. In the other environments, /i/ is represented as [i], but when /i/ follows /l/, it should be noted that both [li] and [ɿ] are phonetically possible. For example, for the word 里 *li* 'inside', the pronunciations [li] and [ɿ] are both found in my data.[1]

Other phonemic vowels are listed and exemplified in (9).

(9) a /y/: [tɕy] 租 'rent'
  b /ɨ/: [pɨ] 背 'back'
  c /ɯ/: [tsɯ] 走 'walk'
  d /u/: [fu] 书 'book'
  e /ɤ/: [tʂʰɤ] 车 'car'
  f /ɛ/: [tɛ] 带 'and'
  g /ɔ/: [xɔ] 好 'good'
  h /a/: [ta] 大 'big'

2.2.2 Nasal vowels

As shown in (10), there are six nasal vowels in Zhoutun.

(10) a /ĩ/: [tɕĩ] 金 'gold'
  b /ỹ/: [ỹ] 云 'cloud'
  c /ũ/: [sũ] 送 'give'
  d /ɤ̃/: [ɻɤ̃] 人 'people'
  e /ã/: [tɕʰiã] 钱 'money'
  f /ɑ̃/: [tɕʰiɑ̃] 藏 'hide'

10 *Phonology*

The first five nasal vowels all have a corresponding oral vowel. The last one, /ã/, has no oral counterpart. The difference between /ã/ and /ã̃/ corresponds in Mandarin Chinese to the contrast between [an] and [aŋ]. For other pairs of alveolar vs. velar nasal of Mandarin Chinese, there is no corresponding contrast in Zhoutun. For example, while Mandarin Chinese has a contrast between /in/ (e.g., [tɕʰin] 'kiss') and /iŋ/ (e.g., [tɕʰiŋ] 'light'), such a contrast is not found in Zhoutun.

2.2.3 Vowel sequences

Zhoutun has 14 vowel sequences, all of which have the second vowel as the primary vowel. They are listed in (11).

(11)   a   /ia/:   [tɕia]   家 'family'
      b   /iã/:   [miã]   面 'flour'
      c   /iã̃/:   [liã̃]   两 'two'
      d   /iɔ/:   [tiɔ]   掉 'drop'
      e   /iɛ/:   [tɕiɛ]   姐 'sister'
      f   /iɯ/:   [iɯ]   有 'have'
      g   /uã/:   [tʂhuã]   穿 'wear'
      h   /ua/:   [xua]   画 'picture'
      i   /uã̃/:   [uã̃]   往 'toward'
      j   /uɛ/:   [xuɛ]   坏 'broken'
      k   /uɤ/:   [uɤ]   饿 'hungry'
      l   /ui̵/:   [tsui̵]   最 'most'
      m   /yã/:   [yã]   远 'far'
      n   /yɤ/:   [yɤ]   药 'herbal'

2.3 Word tones

As a Sinitic variety, Zhoutun is expected to have a tone system. Two phonemic tones are present at first glance, namely, low-rise tone (or 13) and high tone (or 55). Each tone finds some rough correspondence in Middle Chinese. However, for disyllabic phrases, the pattern of tone sandhi is not predictable at the light of Middle Chinese phonology and the synchronic grammatical structure of Zhoutun—two primary factors that determine the patterns of tone sandhi in Chinese—but rather shows a more rigid "low-high vs. high-low" pattern, with "low-high" being more frequent than "high-low". In other words, the phonemic (or syllabic) tones in the tonal system of Zhoutun play a less important role than the "word tones". The word tones are not only largely free from the constraints of the phonemic tones, they also are "coercive" on phonemic tones. For example, even if

花 [xua] 'flower' alone has a low-rise tone (or 13), its tone is low (or 11) in 花瓣 [xua¹¹pã⁵⁵] 'petal' and high (or 55) in 莲花 [liã¹¹xua⁵⁵] 'lotus', both terms having the same low-high word-tone pattern.

In employing tone numbers to describe the tone (Chao 1930), the two phonemic tones low-rise and high can be represented as 13 and 55, and the tone patterns in a disyllabic phrase contain these eight possibilities: 55+11, 11+55, 13+11, 11+13, 13+13, 55+55, 13+55, 55+13. Of these patterns, 11 is not a phonemic tone. In other words, it never appears on a monosyllabic morpheme (the two phonemic tones are 13 and 55). However, when bisyllabic phrases are concerned, 11 bears a role. If we replace 55 with [+high, −low], 13 with [−high, −low] and 11 with [−high, +low], and we use the letter n to represent the number of syllables, the word-tone pattern in Zhoutun can be generalized as $[[-low]_\sigma (n-1)[+low]_\sigma]_\omega$, in which σ stands for syllable and ω for phonological word. The position of [−low] and [+low] syllable has no restriction: the [+low] syllable can precede, follow or occur in the middle of the [−low] syllables. Thus, the word tones in Zhoutun can be summarized as follows:

(12)　1　if n = 1, the word tone is [−low]
　　　　　a　55 [tɕʰi⁵⁵] 去 'go'
　　　　　b　13 [xua¹³] 花 'flower'
　　　2　if n = 2, the word tone is
　　　　2.1 [[−low] [+low]]
　　　　　a　13+11: [tʂhã¹³tɕʰyã¹¹] 长圈 'glow of sun and moon'
　　　　　b　55+11: [tʰɛ⁵⁵iɛ¹¹] 太爷 'grandfather's father'
　　　　2.2 [[+low] [−low]]
　　　　　a　11+13: [a¹¹iɛ¹³] 阿爷 'grandfather'
　　　　　b　11+55: [liã¹¹xua⁵⁵] 莲花 'lotus'
　　　3　if n = 3, the word tone is
　　　　3.1 [[−low] [+low] [+low]]
　　　　　a　55+11+11: [iɛ⁵⁵pɨ¹¹fu¹¹] 夜白蝠 'bat'
　　　　　b　13+11+11: [lɛ¹³xa¹¹ma¹¹] 癞蛤蟆 'toad'
　　　　3.2 [[+low] [−low] [+low]]
　　　　　a　11+13+11: [tʂu¹¹tsi¹³tsʰɔ¹¹] 竹子草 'reed'
　　　　　b　11+55+11: [pɨ¹¹tɯ⁵⁵ɕĩ¹¹] 北斗星 'big dipper'
　　　　3.3 [[+low] [+low] [−low]]
　　　　　a　11+11+13: [xuã¹¹fu¹¹lã¹³] 黄鼠狼 'weasel'
　　　　　b　11+11+55: [mi¹¹ɕy¹¹ua⁵⁵] 女婿娃 'son-in-law'

The situation in which $n > 3$ is rarely seen. From the previous example, we can see that the phonemic tone in Zhoutun is subjected to be reinterpreted in terms of word tones: a syllable whose tone is 13 or 55 (i.e., [−low])

12 *Phonology*

can be used as a single word that is, in most cases, a "minimum free form" (Bloomfield 1933) or "may constitute a complete unterrance, all by itself" (Dixon and Aikhenvald 2003), such as the *xua*[13] 'flower' and *tɕhi*[55] 'go' in (12). It is thus possible to operationally define an *n*-syllable phrase a phonological word when the number of [−low] tone (13 or 55) is one. In other words, an *n*-syllable phonological word constitutes only one [−low] syllable and (*n*-1) [+low] syllable(s).

For a two-syllable phonological word, four types of word tone can be found: 11+13, 11+55, 13+11 and 55+11. They can be divided by the position of 11, as 11-X and X-11, and further as [+low]- [−low] and [−low]-[+low]. Of these two latter types, [+low]- [−low] overwhelmingly outnumbers [−low]-[+low]: among the 590 randomly selected phonological words, 477 (80.8 percent) are [+low]- [−low] and 113 (19.2 percent) are [−low]-[+low]. Further distributions show that 11–55 ([+low]-[+high]), with 307 occurrences, is the main representation of [+low]-[−low] and 55–11 ([+high]-[+low]) is the main representation of [−low]-[+low], whose number of occurrences is 109. From these observations we can conclude that the word tones of Zhoutun are developing toward the pattern "low-high" and "high-low" with "low-high" as a dominant manifestation. The occurrences of tone 13 will probably gradually decrease and the tone in question will be replaced by 55 in phonological words. This is also the case of three-syllable phonological words: among the 63 three-syllable phonological words I recorded, the dominant pattern is 11+55+11/low-high-low, with 35 occurrences; and the number of words with a 13 tone is 11, i.e., less than 18 percent.

2.4 R-ization and reduplication

2.4.1 r-ization

The *r*-ization (see 3.2.1) of Zhoutun is governed by two rules, depending on the type of rhyme.

(13) In a syllable (C) V_1 (V_2):
    1 if V_1 is /i/ or /ĩ/, then the entire rhyme becomes /iɛ/, regardless of the presence of V_2. For example, [ɕiã] > [ɕiɛ] 锹儿 'spade'; [lĩ] > [liɛ] 领儿 'collar';
    2 if V_1 is not /i/ or /ĩ/, then
       a if there is a V_2, then V_2 becomes /ɤ/ and V_1 remains unchanged. For example, [tsuɨ] > [tsuɤ] 嘴儿 'mouth';

b   if there is no V₂, then
   i   when V₁ is /ũ/, it becomes /uɤ/, as in [lũ] > [luɤ] 笼儿 'cage';
   ii   when V₁ is different from /ũ/, it becomes /ɤ/, as in [tsɔ] > [tsɤ] 枣儿 'jujube'.

2.4.2 Reduplication

Reduplication is the repetition of a syllable, where the latter syllable is often accompanied by an *r*-ization in Zhoutun. Two cases are listed here.

The first case, reduplication without *r*-ization, is divided into two categories according to whether it forms a phonological word, e.g., 伯伯 [pa¹¹pa¹³] 'father's brother' and 咕咕 [ku⁵⁵ku⁵⁵] 'cricket'.

The second case of reduplication accompanied by *r*-ization can also be divided into two categories according to whether it forms a phonological word, e.g., 滩滩儿 [tʰã¹¹tʰɤ¹³] 'beach, riverbank' and 柜柜儿 [kuɨ⁵⁵kuɤ¹³] 'cupboard'.

2.5 Syllable structure

The basic syllable structure of Zhoutun is C(V₁)V₂(T). /i/, /u/ and /y/ are the vowels that can appear in V₁ position, while all vowels can appear in V₂ position. Vowels alone can sometimes constitute syllables of the type (V₁) V₂, such as 啊 [a] 'dative-accusative marker' and 外 [uɛ] 'outside'. The tone here stands for the word tone, as discussed earlier. Not every syllable has a surface phonemic tone.

Note

1   The surname 李 *li* is exclusively represented as [ɻ̩] in my data, but since *li* 'inside' can be realized both as [li] and [ɻ̩], I do not consider [ɻ̩] to be an independent phoneme.

3 Nouns and noun phrases

3.1 Definition

Nouns in Zhoutun have two main characteristics. First, they typically function as arguments, commonly including subject, object (direct or indirect object) and as prepositional objects. For example:

(1) a 扎西鸡娃宰下了个。
       tʂaɕi   tɕiua   tsɛ=xɤ=lɔ   kɤ.
       PN   chicken   kill=COMP=PFV   PART
       'Zhaxi killed the chicken.'
   b 我扎西啊打下了。
       ŋɤ   tʂaɕi=a   ta=xɤ=lɔ.
       1   PN=ACC   hit=COMP=PFV
       'I hit Zhaxi.'
   c 我扎西啊东西没心买给。
       ŋɤ   tʂaɕi=a   tũɕi   mɔ   ɕĩ   mɛ=ki.
       1   PN=ACC   stuff   NEG   heart   buy=VIM
       'I did not want to buy anything for Zhaxi.'
   d 箇厨厨里挖了挖，钱儿没哩。
       kuɤ   tʂhutʂhu=li[1]   ua=lɔ   ua,   tɕhiɛ   mi   li.
       3   pocket=LOC   hollow=PFV   hollow   money   NEG   PART
       'S/he hollowed out from pocket, (and find that) there is no money.'
   e 扎西老板 re
       tʂaɕi   lɔpã   ʑi.
       PN   boss   COP
       'Zhaxi is the boss.'

Second, nouns in Zhoutun can be followed by enclitic postpositions, as also shown in (1b, 1c, and 1d).

Although these two are the main factors for determining nouns in Zhoutun, there are also a number of criteria that can assist in identifying a noun, including the following:

DOI: 10.4324/9781003219361-3

Nouns and noun phrases 15

1 A noun can occur in a "(demonstrative) + number + classifier + noun" construction (e.g., (个) 一个人 *(kɤ) i=kɤ ʤ̃* (this) one CL people '(this) one person') or a "noun + number + classifier" construction (e.g., 人一个 *ʤ̃ i=kɤ* people one CL 'one person'). These two constructions are sometimes reduced to "demonstrative + noun" (e.g., 个人 *kɤ ʤ̃* this people 'this person') and "noun + classifier" (e.g., 人个 *ʤ̃ kɤ* people CL 'one person'). For further information about numbers, quantifiers, demonstratives and classifiers, refer to the corresponding sections in the book;
2 A noun may undergo reduplication and *r*-ization, as discussed in the previous section;
3 A noun can be modified by an adjective, another noun and/or a relative clause;
4 A noun can receive a set of specific prefixes and suffixes.

None of the previous criteria alone is a sufficient condition for establishing that a word is a noun, but rather it should be understood that the more of the criteria a word can meet, the closer it is to a noun.

3.2 Word formation

3.2.1 Affixation

Zhoutun affixes can be distinguished into prefixes and suffixes. Prefixes include 老 *lɔ*- '(lit.) old', 初 *tʂhu*- '(lit.) initial', 第 *ti*-, and 阿 *a*-. Suffixes include 子 *-tsi* '(lit.) kid', 娃 *-ua* '(lit.) kid', 儿 *-r* '(lit.) son', and 头 *-thu* '(lit.) head'. Each of these affixes is discussed here.

I. *lɔ*- 老. There are two contexts in which *lɔ*- occurs: it can be used before a monosyllabic noun/morpheme or before a numeral (lower to ten) to create a form with an ordinal meaning. For example:

(2) a 老虎 *lɔxu* 'tiger';   老鼠 *lɔfu* 'rat';   老师 *lɔsi* 'teacher';
    b 老大 *lɔta* 'the eldest';   老二 *lɔr* 'the second';   老三 *lɔsã* 'the third';

II. *tʂhu*- 初. This prefix is used before numerals, mainly for creating expressions that refer to lunar time and the number of years in junior high school. For example:

(3) 初一 *tʂhu-i* 'first day of lunar month/first grade in junior middle school'

Because of the original meaning of *tʂhu*- ('initial'), in expressing lunar time, the numeral after *tʂhu*- is usually not higher than 十 *ʂi* 'ten', and if it is,

16 *Nouns and noun phrases*

it is directly expressed by *ʂi* + numeral, as is 二月十五 *rʏ ʂi u* two month ten five 'the 15th day of the 2nd lunar month'.

III. *ti-* 第. This prefix is the productive marker of the ordinal numerals. See (4).

(4) 第一/十/一百零二 *ti-i/ ʂi/ i pi lĩ r* 'the first/ tenth/ one hundred and second'

IV. *a-* 阿. The function of *a-* in Zhoutun is twofold: first, it is a prefix used with nouns denoting relatives; second, it occurs in interrogative pronouns. For example:

(5) a 阿爷 *aiɛ* 'grandfather',   阿舅 *atɕiu* 'uncle',   阿娘 *aniã* 'aunt',
        阿大 *ata* 'father',   阿妈 *ama* 'mother';
     b 阿个 *akʏ* 'who',   阿里 *ali* 'where';

V. *-tsi* 子. The suffix *-tsi* also has two functions: (i) it can be added to a noun with some kind of diminutive function; (ii) it serves as a deadjectival or a deverbal nominalizer. See (6).

(6) a 蚊子 *uʏtsi* 'mosquito',   肺子 *fitsi* 'lung',   院子 *yãtsi* 'yard',
        肠子 *tʂhãtsi* 'gut'
     b 剪子 *tɕiãtsi* 'scissors', 凿子 *tsɔtsi* 'chisel', 辣子 *latsi* 'pepper'
        (*tɕiã* [v.] 'scissor'),   (*tsɔ* [v.] 'chisel'), (*la* [adj.] 'spicy')

VI. *-ua* 娃. *ua* in Zhoutun is a noun meaning 'child, son', as in *ta/ka ua* 'eldest/youngest son'. Its grammaticalization *-ua* is a suffix used with two functions: (i) it is attached to nouns referring to animals for indicating animal cubs; (ii) it is used with personal names for indicating the male descendant of the person of the base name. For example:

(7) a 鸡娃 *tɕiua* 'chicken',   狗娃 *kuua* 'dog',   猫娃 *mɔua* 'cat',
        羊娃 *iãua* 'sheep'
     b 扎西娃 *tʂaɕiua* 'Zhaxi (a name)', 玉林娃 *ylĩua* 'Yulin (a name)'

Note that in the function (7a), *-ua* is not restricted to refer to small animals, as suggested by its original meaning of 'child, son'. A derivative in *-ua* may also refer to an adult animal like, for example, *tɕiua* in 鸡娃窝抱着个 *tɕiua uʏ pɔ=tʂʏ kʏ* chicken chicken_hatch=PROG PART 'The hen is sitting on her eggs' or 大狗娃 *ta kuua* 'big dog' and 大猫娃 *ta mɔua* 'big cat'. Thus, one cannot claim that *-ua* is a diminutive marker.

VII. *-ʏ* 儿. This suffix always triggers sound changes (specifically, rhyme changes); see 2.4.1. In the Chinese literature, this sort of sound change triggered by 儿 *er*, the counterpart of *-ʏ* meaning 'son', is termed as 儿化 erhua or "r-ization". As a suffix, -ʅ can follow nouns, just like -tsi and -ua, as in (8).

(8) 梨儿 liɛ 'pear', 　　　　枣儿 tsʅ 'jujube', 　　　　桃儿 thʅ 'peach',
　　苍蝇儿 tshãiɛ 'fly', 　　河滩滩儿 xuʅthãthʅ 'riverbank'

Although it is true that a derivative in -ʅ usually denotes a small referent, showing a possible diminutive function of -ʅ, not all the nouns denoting small referents take -ʅ (see ua 'child) In addition, -ʅ can be attached to nouns that refer to large referents, such as 河滩 xuʅthã 'riverbank'. Thus, like -tsi and -ua, -ʅ is not a (properly) diminutive marker.

VIII. -thu 头. The suffix -thu, which has an abstract meaning, can be added to nouns and verbs/adjectives, as in (9a) and (9b), respectively.

(9) a 石头 ʂithu 'stone', 木头 muthu 'wood', 穗头 suithu 'grain head',
　　　渠头 tɕhythu 'the beginning of a canal'
　　b 说头 ʂuʅthu (ʂuʅ [v.] 'say'), 想头 ɕiãthu (ɕiã [v.] 'think'),
　　　割头 kuʅthu (kuʅ [v.] 'mow'), 好头 xɔthu (xɔ [adj.] 'good')

In (9a), the original meaning of -thu ('head'), is transparent in tɕhythu and suithu, but opaque in most of its derivatives, such as ʂithu and muthu. In (9b), the meaning of -thu is elusive: it nominalizes the precedent verb/adjective with the meaning of 'worth doing' or 'have the possibility to do or to be'. For example, kuʅthu can mean that "(the wheat, growing well) can be mowed".

3.2.2 Reduplication

Reduplication is a common morphological process in Zhoutun. It does not apply exclusively to nominal bases but also to verbal and adjectival bases, as shown in the following examples.

(10) a Nominal base: 　外奶奶 uɛnɛnɛ 'grandmother (maternal line)',
　　　　　　　　　　辫辫儿 piãpiɛ 'pigtail', 　篮篮儿 lãlʅ 'basket'
　　 b Adjectival base: 好好儿 xɔxʅ 'in good manner',
　　　　　　　　　　　慢慢儿 mãmʅ 'slowly', 　热热儿 ʅʐʅ 'hotly'
　　 c Verbal base: 　盖盖儿 kɛkʅ 'lid', 　贴贴 thiɛthiɛ 'tag',
　　　　　　　　　　夹夹 tɕiatɕia 'waistcoat'

As these examples indicate, reduplication, often accompanied by r-ization, has an adverbializing or nominalizing effect with, respectively, adjectival bases and verbal bases. For a bound nominal root (a root that cannot be used as a noun by its own), reduplication makes it to be a free noun. For example, the root 辫 *piã* is not a noun before it undergoes reduplication and *r*-ization (becoming 辫辫儿 *piãpiɛ* 'pigtail').

3.2.3 Compounding

Compound words include two roots that have various semantic/syntactic relations, including coordination, attributive, subject–predicate, and verb–object relations, as exemplified in (11).

(11) a Coordination: 泥沙 *miṣa* 'silt', 尘土 *tṣhɿ̃thu* 'dust',
              鬼怪 *kuikuɛ* 'ghost', 街道 *kɛtɔ* 'street'
    b Attributive relation: 草帽 *tshɔmɔ* 'straw', 冰水 *pĩfɿ* 'cold water',
              布鞋 *puxɛ* 'cloth shoes', 半夜 *pãiɛ* 'midnight'
    c Subject–predicate: 月亮 *yɿliã* 'moon'
    d Verb–object: 过年 *kuɿniɛ* 'next year', 剩饭 *ʂɿ̃fã* 'leftover',
              裹腿 *kuɿthui* 'puttee'

In (11a) the two roots have similar meaning. *Miṣa*, for example, is composed of *mi* 'mud' and *ṣa* 'sand'. The words in (11b) are composed of an attribute and a head noun; see *tshɔmɔ* with *tshɔ* 'grass' and *mɔ* 'hat'. Subject–predicate compound nouns are far less frequent. *yɿliã* is one such a noun with *yɿ* 'moon' and *liã* 'brighten'. (11d) shows verb–object compound nouns. *Kuɿniɛ*, for example, is composed of the verb *kuɿ* 'pass' and the noun *niɛ* 'year' in object function.

A major problem for defining compounding words is the distinction between words and phrases. This is a key problem throughout the study of Chinese, rooted in the fact that the way in which compounding words are formed in Chinese is basically the same as the way a phrase (word 1 + word 2) is constructed. Zhoutun presents the same problem, but compared to Mandarin Chinese, there are two criteria that can help distinguish compound words from phrases in this variety. One is word order. Since Zhoutun has a strict SOV word order, the "V-O" order we may observe in some constructions definitely indicates that we are dealing with a compound noun. In (10d), for example, the word *kuɿniɛ* is the term for 'next year' and not the expression 'passing the lunar new year', while *ʂɿ̃fã* is the term for 'the leftover food', not the expression 'leave some food'. The second criterion is represented by the word tones. Given that word tones serve to identify phonological words (as we saw in Section 2.3), although phonological words and grammatical words are not always overlapping, a sequence of two roots that has a word tone has, per se, a high probability of being a (grammatical) word rather than a phrase.

3.3 Number

Zhoutun has two plural markers: 们 =*mɤ* and 列 =*liɛ*.

3.3.1 =mɤ

=*mɤ* corresponds to the common plural marker 们 *men* of Mandarin Chinese but has a broader distribution than the latter. =*mɤ* can be used in the following contexts.

I. It commonly follows a noun denoting human beings and pronouns. For example:

(12) a 老师们 *lɔsi*=*mɤ* 'teachers',   学生们 *ɕyɻʂɿ*=*mɤ* 'students'
     b 我们 *ŋɤ*=*mɤ* 'we',   你们 *ni*=*mɤ* 'you',
       箇们 *kuɤ*=*mɤ* 'they',   各家们 *kuɻtɕia*=*mɤ* 'selves'

This use of =*mɤ* can also be observed with Chinese *men*, but unlike *men*, Zhoutun =*mɤ* can also mark the reflexive pronoun, as in (13).

(13) 各家们拿去。
     kuɻtɕia=*mɤ*   *tshu*   *tɕhi*.
     self=PL   take   go
     '(You) take (it) by yourselves.'

Note that when =*mɤ* is used, a numeral cannot modify the (pro)noun (14).

(14) a 老师们（*三个）来了。
       lɔsi=*mɤ*   *(*sã=kɤ)*   *lɛ*   *lɔ*.
       teacher=PL   three=CL   come   PFV
       'Three teachers came.'
     b 我们（*两个）一搭走哩。
       ŋɤ=*mɤ*   *(*liã=kɤ)*   *ita*   *tsu*   *li*.
       1=PL   two=CL   together   go   PART
       'We two go together.'

II. =*mɤ* can also be added to nouns denoting (parts of) plants, such as 花 *xua* 'flower', 麦子 *mɛtsi* 'wheat', 庄稼 *tʂuãtɕia* 'crops', etc. For example:

(15) 花们开下了个。
xua=mɤ   khɛ=xɤ=lɔ   kɤ.
flower=PL bloom=COMP=PFV   PART
'The flowers are blooming.'

=mɤ is, however, non-obligatory in this case. And note that the nouns denoting animals cannot be marked by =mɤ, e.g., *马们 *ma=mɤ 'horses', *鸡娃们 *tɕiua=mɤ 'chickens'.

III. =mɤ is non-obligatorily used also after inanimate nouns, both countable (e.g., 碗 uã 'bowl', 衣裳 iʂã 'cloth', 腿子 thuitsi 'leg' and 板凳儿 pãtɤ 'bench') and uncountable (e.g., 天爷 thiãiɛ 'rain', 雾 u 'fog' and 雪 ɕyɤ 'blood'). For example:

(16) a 我碗们啊洗去。
    ŋɤ   uã=ma   ɕi   tɕhi.
    1   bowl=PL:ACC   wash   go
    'I go to wash the bowls.'
   b 天爷们下着没。
    thiãiɛ=mɤ   ɕia=tʂɤ   mi.
    rain=PL   drop=PROG   NEG
    'It is not raining.'

IV. =mɤ can be attached to a personal name for indicating the specific group of people to which a person belongs. See (17).

(17) 扎西们饭吃着个，桑吉们酒喝着个。
tʂaɕi=mɤ fã   tʂhi=tʂɤ kɤ,   sãtɕi=mɤ tɕiu xuɤ=tʂɤ   kɤ.
PN=PL   food eat=PROG PART   PN=PL   wine drink=PROG PART
'Zhaxi's group was eating, and Sangji's group was drinking.'

In (17), tʂaɕi=mɤ and sãtɕi=mɤ do not refer to more than one person called Zhaxi or Sangji, but instead refer to the group of people of which Zhaxi is a member and the group to which Sangji belongs.

V. =mɤ is used after the unmarked coordinated sequences "N_1N_2", where N_1 and N_2 indicate pairs of family members, such as 阿大阿妈 ata ama 'father and mother' and 公公婆婆 kũkũ phɤphɤ 'father-in-law and mother-in-law'. In this case, "N_1N_2=mɤ" may refer to more than one pair of "N_1N_2" (18a) or just one pair of "N_1N_2" with no plural meaning (18b). For example:

(18) a 娃娃的阿大阿妈们我啊周屯话教。
uaua=tʁ   ata   ama=mʁ   ŋa   tʂuthŭxua   tɕiɔ.
child=GEN father   mother=PL   1:DAT   Zhoutun_   teach
                                          vernacular
'The students' fathers and mothers will teach me the Zhoutun.'

b 箇的阿大阿妈们箇啊接去了。
kuʁ=tʁ   ata   ama=mʁ   kua   tɕiɛ   tɕhi   lɔ.
3=GEN   father   mother=PL   3:ACC   take   go   PFV
'His/her father and mother went to take him/her.'

VI. Finally, =mʁ can occur after a noun referring to an object or a person, indicating a general action or a specific group of things or people. For example,

(19) a 阿大阿妈们针线们哈做，劳动着哩呗。
ata   ama=mʁ   tʂʁ̃ɕiã=mʁ=xa   tsi,
father   mother=PL   needle_and_thread=PL=ACC   do
lɔtŭ=tʂʁ   li   pi.
work=PROG   PART   PART
'Fathers and mothers were doing needlework; they were working.'

b 扎西太尕了，青青们假放下时，咃教哩说哩。
tsaɕi   the   ka=lɔ,   tɕhĭtɕhĭ=mʁ   tɕia   fã=xʁ   ɕi,
PN   very   young=PFV   PN=PL   holiday   have=COMP   when
tha   tɕiɔ   li   u   li.
LR²   teach   PART   say   PART
'Zhaxi is too young; when children of Qingqing's age are on vacation,
(he said) he would teach them.'

In (18a), tʂʁ̃ɕiã=mʁ refers to the general action of sewing rather than "needle and thread" in the literal sense, as in the expression tʂʁ̃ɕiã=mʁ=xa tsi 'to make needles and threads'. In (18b), tɕhĭtɕhĭ=mʁ refers to the children of the similar age of Qingqing.

3.3.2 =liɛ

=liɛ is likely from the universal quantifier 一列 iliɛ 'all'. It can follow nouns referring to human beings, animals, plants and objects. For example:

(20) a 人列 ɻʁ̃=liɛ 'people', 学生列 ɕyʁsʁ̃=liɛ 'students',
男子列 nãtsi=liɛ 'men'

b 马列 ma=liɛ 'horses', 狗娃列 kuua=liɛ 'dogs', 鸡列 tɕi=liɛ 'chicken'

c 树列 *fu=liɛ* 'trees',   苹果列 *phĩkuʀ=liɛ* 'apples',
   花列 *xua=liɛ* 'flowers'
d 桌子列 *tʂuʀtsi=liɛ* 'tables',   碗列 *uã=liɛ* 'bowls',
   石头列 *ʂithu=liɛ* 'stones'

Unlike *=mʀ*, *=liɛ* cannot follow a personal pronoun (e.g., *我列 *ŋʀ=liɛ* 'we') and does not have the uses of *=mʀ* indicated earlier in (iii)–(vi).

3.4 Case relations

Zhoutun has a number of postpositional case markers, including dative-accusative 哈/啊 *=xa/=a*, comitative-instrumental 兰 *=lã*, ablative 陀*=tha*, locative 上 *=xã* and 里 *=li*, genitive 的 *=tʀ* and comparative marker 看 *khã*. Each will be taken into account here.

3.4.1 Dative-accusative =xa/=a

Zhoutun shows a dative-accusative syncretism. The form *=xa/=a* plays these two roles. The dative usage is examined first. For example:

(21) *=xa/=a* as a dative marker
  a 我扎西哈书一本给了。
     ŋʀ   tʂaɛi=xa fu   i=pr̃   ki=lɔ.
     1   PN=DAT   book   one=CL give=PFV
     'I gave Zhaxi a book.'
  b 扎西玉林哈衣裳取给。
     tʂaɛi ylĩ=xa   iʂã   tshu=ki.
     PN   PN=DAT   coat   take=VIM
     'Zhaxi takes the coat for Yulin.'
  c 扎西玉林哈说着个。
     tʂaɛi ylĩ=xa   ʂuʀ=tʂʀ   kʀ.
     PN   PN=DAT   say=PROG PART
     'Zhaxi is talking to me.'
  d 我扎西哈岁数大着多。
     ŋʀ   tɛaɛi=xa suifu ta=tʂʀ=tuʀ
     1   PN=DAT   age   old=COMP=much
     'I am much older than you.'
  e 扎西哈钱儿有嘀。
     tʂaɛi=xa tɕhiɛ   iu   ti.
     PN=DAT   money   have PART
     'Zhaxi has money.'

f 扎西哈热着很哩。
   tsaɕi=xa ʮ=tsʐ=xɤ̃ li.
   PN=DAT hot=COMP=very PART
   'Zhaxi feels very hot.'

As a dative marker, =xa/=a expresses a wide range of semantic roles, including the recipient, benefactive, addressee, comparative standard, possessor and experiencer, as shown in (21a)–(21f). By "experiencer", I specifically refer to an animate referent that can convey subjective feelings. Thus, the predicate should either be experiential or reflect the subjective feeling of the subject. This is illustrated by examples (22) and (23).

(22) 扎西*（哈）瞌睡了。
     tsaɕi *(=xa) khuʐsuɨ=lɔ.
     PN*(=DAT) sleepy=PFV
     'Zhaxi was sleepy.'

(23) 扎西（*哈）瞌睡了。
     tsaɕi (*=xa) khuʐsuɨ=lɔ.
     PN (*=DAT) sleep=PFV
     'Zhaxi slept.'

The word *khuʐsuɨ* in Zhoutun can mean "sleepy" and "sleep". When it means "sleepy", the subject must be marked by =xa/=a; in contrast, when it means "sleep", the subject cannot be followed by =xa/a. The difference between the two meanings of *khuʐsuɨ* is that "sleepy" is a subjective feeling, whereas "sleep" is an objective fact. Thus, the subject in (22) is an experiencer, whereas the subject in (23) is not.

Also note that, for the same predicate, only the animate experiencer is marked by =xa/=a, whereas a non-experiencer subject cannot be marked by =xa/a. For example,

(24) a 扎西哈腿子疼着。
       tsaɕi=xa thuɨtsi thɤ̃=tsʐ.
       PN=DAT leg ache=PROG
       'Zhaxi feels an ache in his leg.'
     b 扎西的腿子（*哈）疼。
       tsaɕi=tʐ thuɨtsi (*=xa) thɤ̃.
       PN=GEN leg(*=DAT) ache
       'Zhaxi's leg aches.'

In (24a), the constituent marked by =xa is *tsaɕi* 'Zhaxi', the experiencer of the predicate *thɤ̃* 'ache', whereas *thuɨtsi* 'leg' is unmarked. In (24b), *tsaɕi* tʁ thuɨtsi 'Zhaxi's leg' is the subject, but it cannot be marked by =xa because thuɨtsi 'leg' is not an experiencer and cannot convey subjective feelings.

=xa/=a also serves as an accusative marker, as in (25).

(25) =xa/a as an accusative marker
    a 扎西玉林哈打了。
       tʂaɕi   ylĩ=xa   ta=lɔ.
       PN   PN=ACC beat=PFV
       'Zhaxi has beaten Yulin.'
    b 扎西医院里人哈看去了。
       tʂaɕi   yyã=li   ɻĩ=a   khã   tɕhi=lɔ.
       PN   hospital=LOC person=ACC watch go=PFV
       'Zhaxi went to the hospital to visit the patient.'
    c 苹果哈我一个吃了。
       phĩkuʁ=xa ŋʁ i=kʁ   tʂhi=lɔ.
       apple=ACC 1 one=CL eat=PFV
       'I ate an apple.'

It is not, however, a general accusative marker. The use of =xa/a is linked with these three features: animacy, definiteness and word order. That is, when a patient is high-animate, definite or before the agent (as shown in [25a–c], respectively), =xa/=a is used. Without these conditions, it cannot be used (Zhou 2019a for further details).

Typologically, a dative-accusative syncretism can originate either from accusative extending to dative or vice versa (Næss 2008; Malchukov and Narrog 2008). For Zhoutun, I argue (see Zhou 2019b for details) that =xa/a is prototypically a dative marker which extended its functional domain to that of the accusative.

3.4.2 Comitative-instrumental =lã

Comitative and instrumental are also expressed by a single marker in Zhoutun: =lã. Its comitative and instrumental uses can be seen in (26) and (27), respectively.

(26) =lã as a comitative marker
      我阿奶兰街上去了。
      ŋʁ   anɛ=lã   kɛ=xã   tɕhi=lɔ.
      1   grandmother=COM street=LOC go=PFV
      'I went to the street with grandmother.'

(27) =lã as an instrumental marker
a 你说，嘴兰说呗。
ni ʂuɤ, tsuɨ=lã ʂuɤ pɨ.
2 speak mouth=INS speak PART
'You speak, speak with your mouth.'
b 你筷子兰饭哈吃。
ni khuɛtsi=lã fã=xa tʂhi.
2 chopsticks=INS noodle=ACC eat
'You eat the noodle with chopsticks.'
c 西红柿粮食兰换着个。
ɕixũsi liãʂi=lã xuã=tʂɤ kɤ.
tomato foodstuff=INS exchange=PROG PART
'Using tomatoes to exchange foodstuff.'
d 周屯话兰比林说着个。
tʂuthũxua=lã pilĩ ʂuɤ=tʂɤ kɤ.
Zhoutun_vernacular=INS story say=PROG PART
'Saying a story with Zhoutun vernacular.'
e 脚踮踮兰走着。
tɕyɤ tiãtiã=lã tsu=tʂɤ.
foot tiptoe=INS walk=PROG
'Walking tiptoe.'

In (26), =lã, as a comitative marker, is added to the accompanion *anɛ* 'grandmother', while the accompanee is *ŋɤ* 'I'. In (27), =lã marks various kinds of "instruments", including a body part (*tsuɨ* 'mouth'), an artifact (*khuɛtsi* 'chopsticks'), a concrete object (*ɕixũsi* 'tomato'), an abstract referent (*tʂuthũxua* 'Zhoutun vernacular') and a way of walking (*tiãtiã* 'tiptoe') in (27a–e), respectively.

=lã comes from the numeral two. This is supported by the fact that =lã can be replaced by 两个 *liã kɤ* 'two'+ CL in some situations.

(28) a 我兰街上走。
ŋɤ lã kɛ=xã tsu.
1 two street=LOC go
b 我两个街上走。
ŋɤ liã=kɤ kɛ=xã tsu.
1 two=CL street=LOC go
'We two go to the street.'

And "two" developed into comitative and then into instrumental. This is not a common starting point for the grammaticalization of a comitative marker in the Chinese context (see Zhou 2022 for details).

3.4.3 Ablative =tha

The ablative marker =*tha* conveys the meaning "from". For example:

(29) a 你阿里哒来？
    ni ali=tha   lɛ?
    2   where=ABL come
    'Where are you from?'
  b 我北京哒来。
    ŋɤ pitɕĩ=tha   lɛ.
    1   Beijing=ABL come
    'I come from Beijing.'
  c 个哒西宁怎么啊有哩？
    kɤ=tha   ɕĩnĩ   tʂima iu   li?
    here=ABL   Xining how   exist PART
    'How far is it from here to Xining?'
  d 今儿哒我学生娃的课补给。
    tɕiɛ=tha   ŋɤ ɕyɤʂũa=tɤ   khuɤ   pu=ki.
    today=ABL 1   student=GEN lesson   make_up=VIM
    'From today, I will make up missed lessons for the students.'

As shown in the previous examples, =*tha* can be attached to an interrogative pronoun (29a), a location noun (29b), a demonstrative (29c) or a temporal noun (29d).

3.4.4 Locative =li *and* =xã

=*li* and =*xã* correspond to Mandarin Chinese 里 *li* and 上 *shang*, respectively, considered as "locative postpositions" or even "nouns of locality" in the literature. The locative marker *li* in Gan-Qing dialects underwent a higher degree of grammaticalization than its counterpart in Mandarin Chinese.

The original function of =*li* is to denote location in the interior of a three-dimensional space (30a). In Zhoutun, =*li* further indicates location in a non-three-dimensional space (30b–c) or even no physical space at all (e.g., location in time) (30d–e).

(30) a 鱼鱼缸里有哩呗。
    y   ykã=li   iu   li   pɨ.
    fish fishbowl=LOC   exist PART PART
    'Fish is in the fishbowl.'

    b   劳改里看去了。
           lɔkɛ=li   khã   tɕhi=lɔ.
           labor_camp=LOC see   go=PFV
           'Went to see (someone) in the labor camp.'
    c   路里几辆车停着个。
           lu=li   tɕi=liã   tʂhɤ   thĩ=tʂɤ   kɤ.
           road=LOC several=CL car   stop=PROG PART
           'Several cars are on the road.'
    d   天气预报里天爷下哩说。
           thiãtɕhiypɔ=li   thiãiɛ ɕia li   ʂuɤ.
           weather_forecast=LOC rain   fall PART say
           'The weather forecast says that it is going to rain.'
    e   晌午里一个睡了。
           ʂãu=li   i=kɤ   ʂui=lɔ.
           noon=LOC one=CL sleep=PFV
           '(I) slept at noon.'

The word *ykã* 'fishbowl' in (30a) is a typical three-dimensional space; *lɔkɛ* 'labor camp' per se is also three-dimensional, but in (30b), it is its location rather than its shape that is emphasized. In (30c), *lu* 'road' is not three-dimensional but is a two-dimensional space. In (30d), *thiãtɕhiypɔ* 'weather forecast' is not a physical space, as in (30e) where *ʂã'u* 'noon' relates to time.

As regards =xã, see the following examples:

(31) a   房顶上有哩。
           fãtĩ=xã   iu   li.
           roof=LOC exist PART
           '(Something is) on the roof.'
     b   我庙上去哩。
           ŋɤ miɔ=xã   tɕhi li.
           1   temple=LOC go   PART
           'I am going to the temple.'
     c   我报纸上广告个登去哩。
           ŋɤ pɔtʂhi=xã   kuãkɔ=kɤ   tɤ̃   tɕhi li.
           1   newspaper=LOC advertisement=CL publish go   PART
           'I am going to place an advertisement in the newspaper.'
     d   学习上一点不认真哩。
           ɕyɤɕi=xã   itiã pu ɹɤ̃tʂɤ̃ li.
           study=LOC a.bit NEG hard PART
           '(Someone) does not study hard at all.'

In (31), the constituents marked by =xã are non-typical locations (i.e., they are not three-dimensional locations). The use of =xã with these nouns indicates that it went further under its grammaticalization way as a locative marker.

3.4.5 Genitive =tɤ

Similarly to the locative markers, =tɤ in Zhoutun has an equivalent form in Mandarin Chinese, i.e., the frequently used and multifunctional particle 的 *de*. Compared to *de*, =tɤ in Zhoutun is, however, used more frequently and mandatorily as a genitive marker. In other words, for the genitive constructions in Mandarin Chinese where *de* can be omitted, =tɤ must appear in Zhoutun. For example, while in Mandarin Chinese 我书包坏了 *wo shubao huai le* (1 school bag break PFV) 'My school bag is broken' and 我爸爸死了 *wo baba si le* (1 father die PFV) 'My father died' are acceptable, their versions with Zhoutun morphemes (32) are not in this variety.

(32) a 我*（的）书包坏下了个。
 ŋɤ*(=tɤ)   ʂupɔ   xuɛ=xɤ=lɔ   kɤ.
 1=GEN   school.bag   break=COMP=PFV   PART
 'My school bag is broken.'
 b 我*（的）阿大死了。
 ŋɤ*(=tɤ)   ata   si=lɔ.
 1=GEN   father   die=PFV
 'My father died.'

3.4.6 Comparative khã

Besides with the dative marker =xa/=a, a standard of comparison of a comparative sentence may be expressed in Zhoutun with *khã*.

(33) a 扎西的分数看了嘀，我的分数高哩。
 tʂaɕi=tɤ fɻ̝ʂu   khã=lɔ   ti,   ŋɤ=tɤ   fɻ̝ʂu   kɔ   li.
 PN=GEN   score   look=PFV   PART   1=GEN   score   high   PART
 'My score is higher than Zhaxi's.'
 b 你们的房子看上了，我们的房子大。
 nimɤ=tɤ   fãtsi   khã=xã=lɔ,   ŋɤ=mɤ=tɤ   fãtsi   ta.
 2:PL=GEN house   look=COMP=PFV   1=PL=GEN   house   big
 'Our house is bigger than yours.'

khã is the verb 'look' in Zhoutun, and the construction "A *khã*, B Adj" literally means 'looking at A, B is Adj', which is read with the comparative meaning 'B is more Adj than A'. For example, (33a) literally means "Looking at Zhaxi's score, my score is higher", in which the comparative connotation "My score is higher than Zhaxi's" appears. *khã* is not a typical comparative marker, to be exact. It is a verb as indicated by the fact that it can be followed by the aspect marker =*lɔ*. I discuss it here because "A 'look', B Adj" is a conventionalized construction for comparison and *khã* is its core component.

3.5 Referentiality

Referentiality is "the part of the semantics of a nominal component that reflects its connection to the external referent and is used primarily to determine the extension rather than the connotation of a concept" (Liu 2008, 346). The generic and individual referentiality is discussed here.

3.5.1 Generic

A generic noun (phrase) refers to "a whole class of entities rather than to individual members" (Crystal 2008, 209). In Zhoutun, the bare noun (phrase) often receives a generic reading. For example,

(34) a 熊猫竹子吃。
 ɕiũmɔ tṣutsi tṣhi.
 panda bamboo eat
 'Pandas eat bamboo.'
 b 扎西书念不成哩。
 tṣaɕi fu niã pu tṣhɣ̃ li.
 PN book read NEG available PART
 'Zhaxi is not able to go to school.'

ɕiũmɔ and tṣutsi in (34a) and *fu* in (34b), for example, can have these generic readings: ɕiũmɔ and tṣutsi refer to the class of panda and the class of bamboo; *fu* expresses the generic meaning "study". Bare noun phrases, however, do not necessarily have generic reading. See (35).

(35) a 熊猫竹子吃着个。
 ɕiũmɔ tṣutsi tṣhi=tṣɣ kɤ.
 panda bamboo eat=PROG PART
 'The pandas are eating bamboo.'

b 扎西书两遍念下了。
   tʂaɕi   fu   liã=piã   niã=xɤ=lɔ.
   PN   book   two=CL   read=COMP=PFV
   'Zhaxi read the book twice.'

Unlike in (34a), ɕiũmɔ in (35a) is definite, referring to the panda(s) that are mentioned in previous context as a shared knowledge between the addresser and the addressee. Similarly, *fu* in (35b) denotes a specific book.

3.5.2 Individual

The individual category, as the term implies, refers to an individual unit that can be definite and indefinite. A definite unit is the one that is specific and identifiable to the addressee, while an indefinite entity is one which does not receive a specific identification (Crystal 2008, 133, 241). Let us go through the definite entity first.

As in many other languages, the definite property of a noun is expressed by a demonstrative pronoun: 个 *kɤ* 'this' or 箇 *kuɤ* 'that'.

(36) a 个碗你拿上。
      kɤ   uã   ni   na=xã.
      this   bowl 2   take=COMP
      'You take this bowl.'
   b 箇人来了。
      kuɤ   ʅ̃   lɛ=lɔ.
      that   person come=PFV
      'That person came.'
   c 你我啊个书给。
      ni   ŋa   kɤ   fu   ki.
      2   1:DAT this book give
      'You give me this book.'

Demonstratives in Zhoutun have not developed to definite articles. Their core function is deictic, and not all definite nouns are preceded by a demonstrative.

Now I turn to the indefinite units. There is no indefinite article or other dedicated marker for indefinite meaning in Zhoutun. The classifier 个 =*kɤ* in a construction "N=*kɤ*" has a similar function to that of an indefinite article. I would term =*kɤ* a quasi-indefinite article: although it has not yet developed into a real indefinite article, it has to some extent departed from its original function as a classifier, as evidenced by the following facts. First, the classifier in the construction "noun=classifier" can only be *kɤ*, even if there is a classifier more appropriate for the preceding noun. For example, for the noun 衣裳 *iʂã* 'cloth', the pertinent classifier is 件 *tɕiã*, as in 衣裳一件 *iʂã* i=*tɕiã* 'one cloth'; it is, however, unacceptable to say 衣裳件 *iʂã=tɕiã*. Only 衣裳个 *iʂã=kɤ* is the correct expression. Second, when the noun is followed by a numeral phrase (i.e., numeral + classifier), *kɤ* can still be used within a "N=*kɤ* Num CL" structure, like that in (37).

(37) 菜个啊两个炒给。
     tshɛ=ka   *liã=kɤ*   *tʂhɔ=ki.*
     dishes=*kɤ*:ACC   two=CL   stir-fry=VIM
     'Stir-fry two dishes (for somebody).'

This phenomenon shows that *kɤ* is probably on the grammaticalization way to being an indefinite article. However, *kɤ* is not yet a genuine indefinite article. It is perfectly acceptable to take out *kɤ* in (37), as shown in (38).

(38) 菜（哈）两个炒给。
     tshɛ (=xa)   *liã=kɤ*   *tʂhɔ=ki.*
     dishes=ACC   two=CL   stir-fry=VIM
     'Stir-fry two dishes (for somebody).'

The core role of *kɤ* is that of a classifier, and the quasi-indefinite function is an optional extended function. In (37), for example, the noun *tshɛ* can be interpreted as definite. Suppose, for example, that one has ordered two dishes, and that now s/he is asking to the chef to prepare these two dishes for him/her, *tshɛ* is clearly definite in this context.

Notes

1 Here and henceforth, for convenience, "h" refers to aspirated feature "ʰ" instead of the glottal [h] (there is no [h] in Zhoutun's phonology).
2 *tha* is a special pronoun in Zhoutun; I refer to it as the "locutor-referential pronoun", and I gloss it with LR. See section 6.1.5 for details.

4 Verbs and verb phrases

4.1 Definition

A typical verb in Zhoutun can be operationally defined by the following features.

I. It can be followed by aspect markers such as 了 =lɔ, 着 =tʂɤ and 过 =kuɤ. For example:

(1) 扎西街上去了/过。
tʂaɕi   kɛ=xã   tɕhi=lɔ/=kuɤ.
PN   street=LOC go=PFV/=EXP
'Zhaxi went to the street/has been to the street.'

For more details on aspect markers, refer to Section 4.2.

II. It can be followed by 给 =kɨ (lit. 'give') as a valence increasing marker, expressing a variety of semantic meanings, such as causative. For example:

(2) 我箇啊没进来给。
ŋɤ   kua   mɨ   tɕĩlɛ=kɨ.
1   3:DAT   NEG   come=VIM
'I did not let him/her in.'

A more detailed examination of "V=kɨ" can be found in Section 4.6.

III. It can be followed by a series of directional complements, such as 上=xã 'up', 下=xɤ 'down', 来 =lɛ 'come', 去 =tɕhi 'go', etc., as shown in (3).

(3) 个笔你拿上。
kɤ   pi   ni   na=xã.
this   pen   2   take=COMP
'Take this pen.'

For additional information regarding directional complements, refer to Section 4.5.1.

DOI: 10.4324/9781003219361-4

IV. Its negation can be *pu* V, V=*tʂɤ mɨ* or V=*tɤ ma ʨi*. See Section 4.3.5 for more details on negation.

Just like the definition of nouns, the more of the aforementioned features a word, the more likely it is to be a verb.

4.2 Aspect

Aspect in Zhoutun is expressed by adding a specific marker after the verb. The aspectual markers include: (i) perfective 了=*lɔ*; (ii) future 哩 =*li*; (iii) ingressive 脱 =*thuɤ* and 开 =*khɛ*; (iv) progressive 着 =*tʂɤ*; (v); resultative 罢 =*pa* and (vi) experiential 过 =*kuɤ*. Each of them is discussed here.

4.2.1 Perfective

The Zhoutun perfective marker =*lɔ* basically corresponds to *le₁* in Mandarin Chinese.¹ The use of =*lɔ* is shown in the following sentences.

(4) Q: 你阿里去了？
    ni   ali   tɕhi=lɔ?
    2   where go=PFV
    'Where did you go?'
   A: 我庙上去了。
    ŋɤ   miɔ=xã   tɕhi=lɔ.
    1   temple=LOC go=PFV
    'I went to the temple.'

(5) Q: 你苹果吃了么没？
    ni   phĩkuɤ tʂhi=lɔ mɤ mɨ?
    2   apple eat=PFV DISJ NEG
    'Have you eaten the apple(s) or not?'
   A: 吃了。
    tʂhi=lɔ.
    eat=PFV
    'Yes, I have.'

(6) 早晨的下半天我街上陀来了。
   tsɔʂɤ̃=tɤ   xapãthiã   ŋɤ kɛ=xã=tha   lɛ   lɔ.
   tomorrow=GEN afternoon 1 street=LOC=ABL come PFV
   'I would have come back from the street tomorrow afternoon.'

In examples (4) and (5), the reference point of time is the time of speech, and the events denoted by the verbs *tɕhi* 'go' and *tʂhi* 'eat' have already happened or ended before that point. In contrast, in example (6), the event denoted by the verb *lɛ* 'come', marked by *=lɔ*, is in the future. This clearly demonstrates that *=lɔ* has nothing to do with the "temporal location of an event", as tense markers do (Bhat 1999, 43), and that it is an aspect marker.

=lɔ is usually not directly attached to a verb but is used after the sequence "V=*xã/xɤ*", where *=xã* and *=xɤ* are directional complements, literally meaning "up" and "down", respectively. For example:

(7) 昨儿要啥子一个死上了。
    tshuɤ   iɔʂatʂi   i=kɤ   si=xã=lɔ.
    yesterday   beggar   one=CL   die=COMP=PFV
    'A beggar died yesterday.'

(8) 扎西鸡娃宰下了。
    tʂaɕi   tɕiua   tsɛ=xɤ=lɔ.
    PN   chicken   slaughter=COMP=PFV
    'Zhaxi slaughtered the chicken.'

As *=xã* and *=xɤ* often co-occur with *=lɔ* in the sequence "V=*xã/xɤ=lɔ*", they are gradually acquiring the same function of *=lɔ* used alone, as shown in (8).

(9) a 泥兰捏上了着，圆圆这么捏上。
       mi=lã   niɛ=xã=lɔ=tʂɤ,   yãyɤ   tʂɤmɤ   niɛ=xã.
       mud=INS   pinch=COMP=PFV=PROG   round   this.way   pinch=COMP
       'Pinch it with mud and pinch it roundly like this.'
    b 完下了着，灭下哩呀。
       uã=xɤ=lɔ=tʂɤ,   miɛ=xɤ   li   ia.
       finish=COMP=PFV=PROG   extinguish=COMP   PART   PART
       '(The fire) was gone, it would go out.'

In (9a) and (9b), *=xã* and *=xɤ* occur before *=lɔ*, but it should be noted that these two morphemes can also be used alone without *=lɔ* functioning to some extent as perfective markers.

4.2.2 Future

The future aspect indicates that an event will occur after the reference point of time and is marked by the final particle 哩 *=li*. For example:

(10) Q: 你阿里去哩？
         ni   ali   tɕhi   li?
         2   where   go   PART
         'Where are you going to?'

```
A:   我庙上去哩。
     ŋɤ    miɔ=xã        tɕhi    li.
     1     temple=LOC    go      PART
     'I am going to the temple.'
```

(11) 我饭吃了，嘚碗洗去哩。
```
      ŋɤ    fã      tʂhi=lɔ,    tɤ    uã       ɕi=tɕhi        li.
      1     food    eat=PFV     DM    bowl     wash=COMP      PART
      'I have eaten, and I am going to wash the bowl.'
```

Examples (10) and (4), in 4.2.1, form a minimal pair that clearly shows that =*li* conveys a future meaning, in contrast to the perfective =*lɔ*. Example (11) contains both =*lɔ* and =*li* within the same sentence.

Two points should be noted. First, like =*lɔ*, =*li* is an aspectual marker rather than a tense marker. This is indicated by the fact that =*li* can be used in past time. Second, =*li* is not properly a dedicated future marker: the prototypical use of =*li* in Zhoutun is that as a final particle. It is mainly used in declarative sentences to express the tone of a statement, exclamation, etc.[2] See Section 6.6.3 for details.

4.2.3 Ingressive

The ingressive aspect indicates the beginning of a situation. Zhoutun has two ingressive markers which have a slight semantic difference: 脱 =*thuɤ* and 开 =*khɛ*. For example:

(12) a   天爷下脱了。
```
          thiãiɛ        ɕia=thuɤ=lɔ.
```
      b   天爷下开了。
```
          thiãiɛ        ɕia=khɛ=lɔ.
          rain          fall=ING=PFV
          'It has started to rain.'
```

(13) a   水果进着上来，卖脱了。
```
          ʂuikuɤ       tɕĩ=tʂɤ=ʂãlɛ,         mɛ=thuɤ=lɔ.
```
      b   水果进着上来，卖开了。
```
          ʂuikuɤ       tɕĩ=tʂɤ=ʂãlɛ,         mɛ=khɛ=lɔ.
          fruit        stock=COMP=up         sell=ING=PFV
          'The fruit was stocked and began to be sold.'
```

Although both =*thuɤ* and =*khɛ* have basically an ingressive meaning, V=*thuɤ* covers exactly the starting point of the situation indicated by the verb, while V=*khɛ* covers not only the starting point of the situation indicated by the verb but also the short period that follows. For example, (12a) can only mean that the rain has just begun to fall, while (12b) can mean that the rain has been falling for some time, but in practice, it also mean that the rain has just begun to fall. The same applies to the two sentences in (13).

Both =*thuɤ* and =*khɛ* are selected based on the type of situation the verb describes, i.e., the verbs they are attached to cannot denote an event that is completed instantaneously. In other words, the verbs cannot be non-durative verbs, such as *si* 'die'. In addition, =*khɛ* cannot be attached to a verb denoting an abstract action. For example:

(14) 学里去脱/*开时嘚街上去哩。
  ɕyɤ=li   tɕhi=thuɤ/*=khɛ   ʂi   tɤ   kɛ=xã   tɕhi li.
  school=LOC go=ING/=ING   when DM street=LOC go PART
  'When someone begins to go to school, s/he is going to the street (where the school is located).'

The verb *tɕhi* 'go' is abstract in the sense that it denotes no specific manner of moving, and =*khɛ* cannot be used with it because one cannot say "s/he started to go and the 'go' lasted for a while". Verbs with more specific meanings like *tsu* 'walk' and *phɔ* 'run' may instead be attached by =*khɛ*.

4.2.4 Progressive

Progressive marker 着 =*tʂɤ* indicates that a given event is in progress at the reference point of time. For example:

(15) 雪花飘着个。
  ɕyɤxua   phiɔ=tʂɤ   kɤ.
  snowflake float=PROG PART
  'The snowflakes are floating in the sky.'

(16) 箇们几个人一列街上话攀着。
  kuɤ=mɤ tɕi=kɤ   .tʐ̃   iliɛ kɛ=xã   xua   phã=tʂɤ.
  3=PL several=CL people all street=LOC words chat=PROG
  'They are all chatting on the street.'

(17) 菜个啊两个炒了着。
  tshe   ka   liã=kɤ   tʂhɔ=lɔ=kɤ.
  dish   CL:ACC two=CL   fry=PFV=PROG
  'The dishes were stir-fried.'

(18) 个菜香着嘀。
  kɤ   tshe   ɕiã=tʂɤ   ti.
  this dish   fragrant=PROG PART
  'This dish smells good.'

(19) 玉林的娃哈文鑫叫着嘀。
    ylĩ=tɤ   ua=xa   uɹ̃ɕĩ   tɕiɔ=tʂɤ   ti.
    PN=GEN child=DAT PN   call=PROG   PART
    'Yulin's child is called Wenxin.'

In examples (15) and (16), =tʂɤ marks actions ('float' and 'chat') that are in progress. In (17), =tʂɤ is used after the perfective marker =lɔ, forming a "V=PFV=PROG" construction, indicating that the action denoted by the verb tʂhɔ 'fry' occurred and continued. Example (18) shows that =tʂɤ can also be attached to an adjective. In (19), the verb tɕiɔ 'call' describes a transient action. Unlike phiɔ 'float' and phã 'chat', tɕiɔ is not a typical verb that can be used in the progressive.

In addition to being a progressive marker, =tʂɤ can also be used as a complement marker equivalent to 得 de in Mandarin Chinese; see Section 4.5 for more details.

4.2.5 Resultative

The resultative aspect indicates the successful completion of a situation (Comrie 1976, 20). The resultative marker in Zhoutun is 罢 =pa. For example:

(20) 花一遍开罢，挖出，靠埋上，开罢了，个第二茬。
    xua   i=piã   khɛ=pa,   ua=tʂhu,   khɔ   mɛ=xã,
    flower one=CL open=RES   dig=OUT   again bury=COMP
    khɛ=pa=lɔ,   kɤ   tsi=ɤ   tʂha.
    open=RES=PFV this   ORD=two stubble
    'The flowers were bloomed once; they were dug out and buried again. They were bloomed and this is the second time.'

(21) 热罢了。
    ɹɤ=pa=lɔ.
    hot=RES=PFV
    'It has been heated.'

(22) 我们席吃罢了，上来了。
    ŋɤ=mɤ   ɕi   tʂhi=pa=lɔ,   ʂãlɛ=lɔ.
    1=PL   banquet eat=RES=PFV come=PFV
    'We finished the banquet and came up (referring to going home).'

The resultative marker =pa often co-occurs with the perfective marker =lɔ because the semantics of "result" and "accomplish" are close. We must note, however, that while =pa focuses on the point at which a bounded event ends,

=lɔ indicates that an event has already started or that the state of "the event has happened" has been reached. In (20), for example, *khɛ* 'bloom' refers to the end point of the bounded event "the flower blooms", an event which theoretically has a beginning and an end point. The use of =*pa* highlights the end of the event. In contrast, if =*lɔ* is used, the "bloom" is reduced to a point and it is emphasized that the "bloom" has already occurred before the reference point of time or that the "blooming" state has already been reached.

4.2.6 Experiential

The experiential aspect, marked by =*kuʐ*, indicates that a given situation has held at least once during some time in the past leading up to the present (Comrie 1976, 58). Unlike perfective, the perspective of this aspect is that of the subject (usually a person) who experiences an event, rather than the event itself. For example,

(23) 你街上去过了么没？
 ni   kɛ=xã   tɕhi=kuʐ=lɔ   mʐ   mi?
 2   street=LOC go=EXP=PFV   DISJ   NEG
 'Have you been to the street or not?'

(24) 我车没学过呀，开不来。
 ŋʐ   tʂhʐ   mi   ɕyʐ=kuʐ   ia,   khɛ=pu=lɛ.
 1   car   NEG   learn=EXP   PART   drive=NEG=COMP
 'I have never learned to drive, (so) I cannot drive.'

4.2.7 The expression of tense

Zhoutun has no dedicated tense markers; instead, aspect markers are used to express the tense meaning. For example, perfective =*lɔ* and experiential =*kuʐ* can be used to express the past tense, =*tʂʐ* roughly assumes the function of present tense, and =*li* can be used to express the future tense.[3] As the core function of these markers is to express the aspect meaning and tense is only a secondary function, the latter meaning is essentially inferred pragmatically and can be discarded in certain contexts. For example, the reason the perfective marker =*lɔ* is basically used to express a past situation is due to its aspectual meaning, which is pragmatically in line with past tense. Nevertheless, =*lɔ* can be used to express a future situation, which makes it essentially different from a past tense marker.

Bhat (1999) explored the possibility of dividing languages in terms of the prominence of tense, aspect and mood, into tense-prominent, aspect-prominent and mood-prominent languages. A tense/aspect/mood-prominent language tends to express the other two categories by prominent tense/aspect/mood distinctions. Liu (2012a) pointed out that aspect in Chinese is prominent and extends to tense, which is also the case in Zhoutun.

4.3 Modality

4.3.1 Dynamic modality

Dynamic modality "relates to ability and willingness" (Palmer 2001, 10). In Zhoutun, the abilitative modality is expressed by the verb-complement construction V=*lε*, in which =*lε* is a directional complement literally meaning "come". For example,

(25) Q: 扎西，你车开来哩么？
      tşaɕi,   ni   tşhɤ   khɛ=lɛ   li   mɤ?
      PN   2   car   drive=COMP PART Q
      'Zhaxi, can you drive?'
   A: 开来哩。
      khɛ=lɛ   li.
      drive=COMP PART
      'I can drive.'

(26) 个猫娃老鼠抓来了个。
    kɤ   mɔua   lɔtşhu   tşua=lɛ=lɔ   kɤ.
    this   cat   rat   catch=COMP=PFV PART
    'This cat could catch rats.'

(27) 㑇我周屯话一点点说来了。
    tɤ   ŋɤ   tşuthũxua   itiãtiã   şuɤ=lɛ=lɔ.
    DM   1   Zhoutun.vernacular little   speak=COMP=PFV
    'I can speak a little Zhoutun vernacular.'

Note that the construction V=*lε* can also express the directional meaning of "come and V"; see the discussion of the serial verb construction in Section 4.4.

The negation of the modal construction V=*lε* is V=*pu*=*lε*, where the negative marker *pu* is inserted between V and =*lε*, as in the following examples:

(28) 我字写不来。
    ŋɤ   tsi   ɕiɛ=pu=lɛ.
    1   character write=NEG=COMP
    'I cannot write.'

(29) 丫头太尕了，还话说不来。
 iathu thε ka lɔ, xã xua ʂuɤ=pu=lε.
 girl too young PART still words speak=NEG=COMP
 'Being too young, the girl cannot speak yet.'

Besides the V=*lε* construction, Zhoutun also uses the verb-complement constructions V=*xã* (where 上 *xã* literally means 'up') and V=*xɤ* (where 下 *xɤ* means 'down') for the modal meaning of ability. Similarly, the negation of V=*xã* and V=*xɤ* are V=*pu=xã* and V=*pu=xɤ*, respectively, but, unlike V=*lε*, there is another means of negating V=*xã* and V=*xɤ*, i.e., V=*xã/xɤ=tɤ ma ʨi*. For example:

(30) Q: 连珺一顿上三碗吃上哩么？
 liãtɕẽ i=tũ=xã sã uã tʂhi=xã li mɤ?
 PN one=CL=LOC three bowl eat=COMP PART Q
 'Can Lianjun eat three bowls in one meal?'
 A: 吃上的 ma re。
 tʂhi=xã=tɤ ma ʨi.
 eat=COMP=NOMZ NEG COP
 'She cannot.'

(31) Q: 个包包儿重着很哩，你拿动下哩么？
 kɤ pɔpɤ tʂhũ=tʂɤ=xɤ̃ li, ni na=thũ=xɤ li mɤ?
 this bag heavy=COMP=very PART 2 take=move=COMP PART Q
 'This bag is so heavy. Can you carry it?'
 A: 我拿动下哩。
 ŋɤ na=thũ=xɤ li.
 1 take=move=COMP PART
 'I can carry it.'

(32) 个钱儿打不上哩。
 kɤ tɕhiε ta=pu=xã li.
 here money send=NEG=COMP PART
 'The money cannot be sent in this place.'

(33) 扎西今晚夕来不下，车没哩。
 tʂaɕi tɕĩ uãɕi lε=pu=xɤ, tʂhɤ mi li.
 PN today evening come=NEG=COMP car NEG PART
 'Since there is no means of communication tonight, Zhaxi cannot come here.'

Although all three constructions can convey ability, there are slight differences between V=*lε* and V=*xã/=xɤ*. Specifically, V=*lε* tends to denote an internal capacity possessed by the subject in a stable manner, while V=*xã/ xɤ* tends to express a momentary capacity that is constrained by external conditions. This difference is clear when one takes into account their negative forms. For example, to express "I cannot carry the bag", the expression *na=pu=thũ=xɤ* emphasizes that the bag is too heavy and that it leads me to fail to carry it. In other words, the heaviness of the bag is the external condition that constrains "my" ability to carry it. In contrast, the expression *na=pu=lɛ* recalls another situation, such as "I was too young and strengthless", which is an internal, stable capacity for the subject.

We now turn to volitive modality. There are two strategies in Zhoutun for expressing willingness, namely, the use of 我的心有/没 "V=*tɤ ɕĩ iɯ/mɨ*" or 莫心 V "*mɔ ɕĩ* V". Each is discussed here.

The "V=*tɤ ɕĩ iɯ/mɨ*" strategy firstly places a verb into a "V=*tɤ ɕĩ*" construction, which literally means "the heart to V", a means of expressing willingness. The addition of *iɯ/mɨ* 'have/not have' convey that the subject has or has no willingness to do something. For example:

(34) 扎西车学的心有个。
    tsaɕi   tshɤ   ɕyɤ=tɤ   ɕĩ   iɔ   kɤ⁴.
    PN   car   learn=REL   heart   have   PART
    'Zhaxi wants to learn driving.'

Another construction, "*mɔ ɕĩ* V", is restricted to a negative meaning, i.e., there is no positive counterpart "*iɯ ɕĩ* V". An example of this construction is (35).

(35) 扎西我啊东西莫心买给。
    tsaɕi   ŋa   tũɕi   mɔ   ɕĩ   mɛ=kɨ.
    PN   1:DAT   thing   not_have   heart   buy=VIM
    'Zhaxi does not want to buy me a gift.'

4.3.2 Epistemic modality

With epistemic modality, "speakers express their judgments about the factual status of the proposition" (Palmer 2001, 8). Based on the degree of factualness of the proposition judged by speakers, Zhoutun can distinguish between two types of epistemic modality, namely, speculative modality and deductive modality. Speculative modality refers to a low-factualness judgment, while deductive modality refers to a high-factualness judgment. Despite the lack of any specific markers attached to verbs for these modal meanings, Zhoutun uses final particles to indirectly express the two types of modality.

First, the particle 吧 *pa* is used for speculation. For example:

(36) 早晨天晴着哩吧。
　　 tsɔʂʅ̃　　　　thiã　　　 tɕĩ=tʂɤ　　　　li　　　 pa.
　　 tomorrow　　 weather　 sunny=PROG　 PART　 PART
　　 'Tomorrow would possibly be sunny.'

(37) 扎西街上去了吧。
　　 tʂaɕi　　 kɛ=xã　　　　 tɕhi=lɔ　　 pa.
　　 PN　　　 street=LOC　　 go=PFV　　 PART
　　 'Zhaxi possibly went to the street.'

Second, the particle 嘀 *ti* is used for deduction. For example,

(38) 扎西街上去了嘀。
　　 tʂaɕi　　 kɛ=xã　　　　 tɕhi=lɔ　　 ti.
　　 PN　　　 street=LOC　　 go=PFV　　 PART
　　 'Zhaxi probably went to the street.'

(39) 玉林碗洗着嘀。
　　 ylĩ　 uã　　　 ɕi=tʂɤ　　　 ti.
　　 PN　 bowl　　 wash=PROG　 PART
　　 'Yulin is probably washing the bowls.'

Comparing (37) and (38), it is clear that with the use of *pa*, the proposition "Zhaxi went to the street" is just a guess (with low possibility) for the speaker, whereas with the use of *ti*, this proposition has a much higher chance of being true based on the speaker's judgment.

For more information on the uses of the particle *pa* and *ti*, see Section 6.6.

4.3.3 Deontic modality

The deontic modality is generally divided into the permissive, the obligative and the commissive modalities (Palmer 2001). In Zhoutun, none of these meanings has a special grammatical marker. Instead, only certain unsystematic strategies are employed for these three values.

First, for the permissive meaning, Zhoutun uses the construction V 时不成 "V ʂi (pu) tʂhɤ̃", in which *ʂi* means 'if' (< 'when' < 'time') and *tʂhɤ̃* means 'able', and the whole structure literally means "if V, it is (not) permitted". For example:

(40) 唓你去时成嘀。
　　 tɤ　 ni　 tɕhi　 ʂi　 tʂhɤ̃　 ti.
　　 DM　 2　 go　　 if　 able　　 PART
　　 'Now you can go.'

(41) 你饭吃时也成嘀，馍馍吃时也成嘀，不吃时不成呀。
 ni   fã   tʂhi ʂi iɛ   tʂhr̃ ti,   mɤmɤ   tʂhi ʂi iɛ
 2   noodle eat   if also able PART steamed_bun eat   if also
 tʂhr̃ ti,   pu   tʂhi ʂi pu   tʂhr̃ ia.
 able PART NEG eat   if NEG able PART
 'You can eat noodles or steamed buns, but you are not permissive to eat nothing.'

Second, Zhoutun uses the adverb 一定玛定 *itĩmatĩ* to express the obligative meaning and for negative obligative meaning (or prohibitive meaning), the construction V 不得 "V=*pu*=*tɤ*" is used. For example:

(42) 娃娃们书一定玛定念着个。
 uaua=mɤ   fu   itĩmatĩ niã=tʂɤ   kɤ.
 child=PL   book   must   read=PROG   PART
 'Children must go to school.'

(43) 箇狗娃有个，娃娃们去不得嘀。
 kuɤ   kuua   iɔ   kɤ,   uaua=mɤ   tɕhi=pu=tɤ   ti.
 there dog   exist   PART   child=PL   go=NEG=COMP   PART
 'There is a dog, and the children must not go there.'

(44) 个烟吃不得。
 kɤ   iã   tʂhi=pu=tɤ.
 here   cigarette   smoke=NEG=COMP
 'It is forbidden to smoke here.'

(45) 法律上规定着，两个媳妇娶不得。
 faly=xã   kuitĩ=tʂɤ,   liã=kɤ   ɕifu   tɕhy=pu=tɤ
 law=LOC   rule=PROG   two=CL   wife   marry=NEG=COMP
 'According to laws, it is forbidden to marry two wives.'

Third, for commissive meaning, the adverb *itĩmatĩ* or the particle *pa* may be used. Specifically, the adverb *itĩmatĩ* may be used to express a definite commitment, while the particle *pa* may be used for a less definite commitment. For example:

(46) 早晨我一定玛定送来哩。
 tsɔʂɤ̃   ŋɤ   itĩmatĩ   sũ   lɛ   li.
 tomorrow   1   must   send   come   PART
 'I will send something tomorrow for sure.'

44 *Verbs and verb phrases*

(47) 早晨我送来哩吧。
　　 tsɔʂɤ̃　　　ŋɤ　sũ　　le　　　li　　pa.
　　 tomorrow　 1　 send　come　PART　PART
　　 'I will send something tomorrow (but I am not so sure about it).'

4.3.4 Evidentiality

Evidentiality relates to the source of the information. Zhoutun has only a single evidential marker, 说 ʂuɤ 'say', indicating the information provided by the sentence in which it occurs is heard from others. ʂuɤ is also an independent transitive verb, as shown in (48).

(48) Q:　扎西什么说着个？
　　　　 tʂaɕi　　sɤ̃mɤ　　ʂuɤ=tʂɤ　　kɤ?
　　　　 PN　　 what　　 say=PROG　PART
　　　　 'What is Zhaxi saying?'
　　 A:　阿吉的钱丢了说。
　　　　 aʨi=tɤ　tɕhiã　　tiu=lɔ　　ʂuɤ.
　　　　 3=GEN　money　lose=PFV　say
　　　　 '(He) said that his money got lost.'

In this example, sɤ̃mɤ is the object of ʂuɤ (Q) and aʨi=tɤ tɕhiã tiu=lɔ its object clause (A). In this context, ʂuɤ is a content verb instead of an evidential marker. But in other contexts, the meaning of 'say' appears to be blurred and the evidential meaning 'it is said that' emerges. We can imagine, for example, that when the answer of (48) is addressed to another hearer who is not on the spot. The reading of the clause is reinterpreted as "It is said that his money got lost", in which the one who said "His money got lost" is not important or becomes unknown.

Here a typical example where ʂuɤ can be interpreted as a pure evidential marker is given:

(49) Q:　个什么 re?
　　　　 kɤ　　sɤ̃mɤ　　ɖi?
　　　　 this　what　　 COP
　　　　 'What is this?'
　　 A:　溜溜球说。
　　　　 liuliutɕiu　　ʂuɤ.
　　　　 yo-yo　　　 EVIDENTIAL
　　　　 'It is a yo-yo.'

In (49), the speaker wanted to know the name of an object that was kept in the hand of a local child and asked Q. The child replied that the object is called a *yo-yo*. Note that no one else on the spot really told the child that the object was called a *yo-yo*. The child used *ʂuʅ* to indicate that the information "It is a yo-yo" is heard from others, and he may not be certain about the truth of the information or he is not responsible for saying it is a yo-yo.

4.3.5 Negation

There are four productive ways to express negation. See the following examples:

(50) X ma re/ 不是 X *ma ȵi/pu ʂi* (X= NP)
    a 个学生 ma re/ 不是呀。
        kʅ   ɕyʅsĩ   ma   ȵi/   pu   ʂi   ia.
        this   student   NEG   COP/   NEG   COP   PART
        'This person is not a student.'
    b 今儿热的 ma re。
        tɕiɛ   ʅʅ=tʅ   ma   ȵi.
        today   hot=NOMZ   NEG   COP
        'Today is not hot.'
    c 扎西饭吃的 ma re。
        tʂaɕi   fã   tʂhi=tʅ   ma   ȵi.
        PN   meal   eat=NOMZ   NEG   COP
        'Zhaxi does not eat the meal.'

This construction is used to negate the noun phrase. Note that the negative copulas *ma re*, borrowed from Amdo Tibetan, and *pu ʂi*, inherited from Chinese, coexist. Comparatively, *ma re* is used far more frequently than *pu ʂi*.

It seems that in (50b) and (50c) *ma ȵi* negates the adjective *ʅʅ* and the verb *tʂhi*, respectively. This is not the case. Due to the use of a nominalizer =*tʅ*, *ʅʅ=tʅ* and *tʂhi=tʅ* could be treated as noun phrases grammatically.

(51) 不 X *pu* X (X= VP or AP)
    a 早晨我不来哩。
        tsɔʂĩ   ŋʅ   pu   lɛ   li.
        tomorrow   1   NEG   come   PART
        'I will not come tomorrow.'
    b 个房子不大哩。
        kʅ   fãtsi   pu   ta   li.
        this   house   NEG   big   PART
        'This house is not big.'

The negator *pu* occurs before verb phrases or adjective phrases. The construction *pu* VP means "not going/willing to VP", while *pu* AP means the negation of the property represented by the adjective phrase.

(52) 没 X *mɨ* X (X= VP)
 昨儿我街上没去。
 tshuʁ   ŋʁ   kɛ=xã   mɨ   tɕhi.
 yesterday   1   street=LOC   NEG   go
 'I did not go to the street yesterday.'

Unlike the construction *pu* VP, the construction *mɨ* VP negates the occurrence of the event represented by the verb phrase. Thus, when negating a verb phrase, *pu* VP is usually used if the event denoted is in a future context, whereas *mɨ* VP is used if the event is in a past context.

(53) X 着没 X=*tʂʁ*=*mɨ* (X= VP or AP)
 a 我扎西啊喜着没哩。
  ŋʁ   tʂaɕi=a   ɕi=tʂʁ=mɨ   li.
  1   PN=ACC   like=PROG=NEG   PART
  'I do not like Zhaxi.'
 b 个房子大着没哩。
  kʁ   fãtsi   ta=tʂʁ=mɨ   li.
  this   house   big=PROG=NEG   PART
  'This house is not big.'

This construction parallels with *pu* VP/AP in that they both can negate a verb phrase and an adjective phrase. The difference is that X=*tʂʁ*=*mɨ* favors adjective phrases and "nontypical" verb phrases (such as static verbs). Thus, comparatively, verb phrases favor *pu* VP constructions and adjective phrases incline to appear in AP=*tʂʁ*=*mɨ* constructions.

4.4 Serial verb constructions

A serial verb construction (SVC) is a syntactic construction in which two or more verb phrases co-occur in a sequence and between them there are no coordinating or subordinating markers. Another key factor determining the identity of an SVC is that the verb phrases denote an integrated event rather than separated, unrelated events (Aikhenvald 2006; Liu 2015). See some examples of SVCs from Zhoutun here.

(54) 阿吉门啊揉开了进来了。
  atɕi   mɹ̃=a   sã=khɛ=lɔ   tɕĩlɛ=lɔ.
  3   door=ACC   push=open=PFV   come=PFV
  'S/he pushed the door open and came in.'

(55) 扎西饭吃上了去了。
　　　tṣaɕi　　　fã　　　tʂhi=xã=lɔ　　　tɕhi=lɔ.
　　　PN　　　meal　　eat=COMP=PFV　　go=PFV
　　　'Zhaxi ate and left.'

(56) 扎西呼拉哩拉哩瞌睡下了着。
　　　tṣaɕi　　xu　　　la=li=la=li　　　　　khuʐsui=xɤ=lɔ=tʂɤ.
　　　PN　　snore　snore=PART=snore=PART　sleep=COMP=PFV=PROG
　　　'Zhaxi snored and fell asleep.'

(57) 牛、羊、马一满跑了出来了个。
　　　niu,　　iã,　　ma　　imã　　phɔ=lɔ　　tʂhulɛ=lɔ　　　kɤ.
　　　cattle　sheep　horse　all　　run=PFV　come.out=PFV　PART
　　　'The cattle, sheep and horses all ran out.'

(58) 连珺跑着过来了。
　　　liãtɕỹ　　phɔ=tʂɤ　　kuʐlɛ=lɔ.
　　　PN　　　run=PROG　come=PFV
　　　'Lianjun is running and coming.'

(59) 饭啊端上了吃。
　　　fã=a　　　　tuã=xã=lɔ　　　　tʂhi.
　　　food=ACC　hold=COMP=PFV　　eat
　　　'Pick up the food and eat.'

These examples all feature the lack of coordinating or subordinating markers between serial verb phrases and denote an integrated event in which the "micro-events" are semantically related. For example, in (54), the two actions "push the door" and "come" constitute a continuous situation. Note that the English translations on each example (except [57]) are not SVCs, due to the use of the coordinator "and".

Aikhenvald (2006, 3) divided SVCs into symmetrical SVCs and asymmetrical SVCs. Symmetrical SVCs "consist of two or more verbs each chosen from a semantically and grammatically unrestricted class", and asymmetrical SVCs "include a verb from a grammatically or semantically restricted class". The unrestricted class of verbs are "major verbs", and the restricted class of verbs are "minor verbs", usually the verbs of motion, posture, etc. The most SVCs in Zhoutun are asymmetrical ones, in which the minor verb usually refers to a directional meaning, such as *lɛ* 'come' and *tɕhi* 'go'. See (54), (55), (57) and (58). Other examples are:

48 *Verbs and verb phrases*

(60) 苹果落着下来了。
phĩkuʁ   luʁ=tʂʁ   ɕialɛ=lɔ.
apple   fall=PROG   come_down=PFV
'The apples fell down.'

(61) 面片一碗一碗端着出来。
miãphiɛ   i=uã=i=uã   tuã=tʂʁ   tʂhulɛ.
mianpian   one=bowl=one=bowl   hold=PROG   come_out
'Bowls of mianpian (a kind of noodle) were held and (the waiter) came out.'

(62) 街上咃一转浪上了上来着嘀。
kɛ=xã=tha   i=tʂuã   lã=xã=lɔ   ʂãlɛ=tʂʁ   ti.
street=LOC=ABL   one=CL   play=COMP=PFV   come=PROG   PART
'(Someone) played around the street and came back.'

(63) 韭菜啊背上了去了。
tɕiutshɛ=a   pɨ=xã=lɔ   tɕhi=lɔ.
leek=ACC   back=COMP=PFV   go=PFV
'(Someone) backed the leeks and went away.'

(64) 我房子里酒个啊两瓶拿了去了。
ŋʁ   fãtsi=li   tɕiu   ga   liã   phĩ   na=lɔ   tɕhi=lɔ.
1   house=LOC   wine   this:ACC   two   bottle   take=PFV   go=PFV
'I took two bottles of wine in the house and went away.'

(65) 我出去了看时，人没呀。
ŋʁ   tʂhutɕhi=lɔ   khã   ʂi,   ɻ̃   mɨ   ia.
1   go_out=PFV   look   when   people   not_have   PART
'When I went out and looked, there were no people.'

(66) 锅啊打着掉了着。
kuʁ=a   ta=tʂʁ   tiɔ=lɔ=tʂʁ.
pot=ACC   knock=PROG   fall=PFV=PROG
'The pot was knocked off the floor.'

As minor verbs, *lɛ* 'come' and *tɕhi* 'go' follow the major verb, as shown by the following examples.

(67) 你饭吃来。
ni   fã   tʂhi   lɛ.
2   meal   eat   come
'You come and eat the meal.'

(68) 衣裳穿来呀。
   iṣã   tṣhuã   lɛ   ia.
   cloth wear   come   PART
   'Come and wear the cloth!'

(69) 我碗取去哩。
   ŋɤ   uã   tshuu   tɕhi   li.
   1   bowl   take   go   PART
   'I am going to take the bowl.'

(70) 个猫娃老鼠抓去了个。
   kɤ   mɔua   lɔtṣhu   tṣua   tɕhi=lɔ   kɤ.
   this   cat   rat   catch   go=PFV   PART
   'This cat went to catch the rat.'

The SVC "V *lɛ/tɕhi*" violates the iconicity principle given that the macro-event it describes is "*lɛ/tɕhi* somewhere and then V". It is not uncommon, however, as argued by Aikhenvald (2006), that the arrangement of the verbs in asymmetrical SVCs violate this principle. The two authors also point out that the minor verbs in an asymmetrical SVC may undergo further grammaticalization, just the case found in "V=*lɛ*" in which =*lɛ* expresses a modal value (abilitative), as we saw in Section 4.3.1.

4.5 Verb-complement constructions

A verb-complement construction is a distinctive construction typically found in Chinese varieties. The term "complement" here does not refer to the complement clause (such as an object clause) but is the translation of 补语 *buyu* 'complementary words'. A "complement" is used to add extra information to the verb. Zhoutun has three subtypes of verb-complement constructions, namely, the verb-direction construction, the verb-result construction and the verb-degree construction.

4.5.1 Verb-direction constructions

Zhoutun has four main directional verbs: 来 *lɛ* 'come', 去 *tɕhi* 'go', 上 *ṣã* 'go up' and 下 *ɕia* 'go down'. These verbs can independently occupy the verb slot. For example:

(71) 你阿里咃来了？
   ni   ali=tha   lɛ=lɔ?
   2   where=ABL   come=PFV
   'Where did you come from?'

50   *Verbs and verb phrases*

(72)   我去哩。
       ŋɤ   tɕhi   li.
       1   go   PART
       'I am going to leave.'

(73)   你不上么？
       ni   pu   ʂã   mɤ?
       2   NEG   up   PART
       'Did not you go home? (lit. Did not you go up?)'

(74)   我下哩。
       ŋɤ   ɕia   li.
       1   down   PART
       'I am going to go to the street. (lit. I am going to go down.)'

The direction of both *lɛ* and *tɕhi* is relative to the direction of the speaker. That is, *lɛ* means "to move forward to the speaker", while *tɕhi* means "to move away from the speaker". Differently, *ʂã* refers to going to a place with relatively higher altitude, and *ɕia* refers to a going to a place with relatively lower altitude. In daily conversations, *ŋɤ ɕia li* usually means "I am going to the county town", and *ŋɤ ʂã li* means "I am going home in the Zhoutun village", just because the altitude of the county town is lower than that of the Zhoutun village. In many Chinese dialects, however, it is the social status of a place that determines the use of the two verbs: "up" to the county town and "down" to the village.

Two of the four directional verbs listed, *lɛ* and *tɕhi*, function as minor verbs in SVCs, as discussed in the previous section. I do not consider these "V *lɛ*" and "V *tɕhi*" constructions as verb-complement constructions. Only a sequence "V=*lɛ*" that expresses modal meaning, as we saw in Section 4.3, can be treated as a verb-complement construction.

As regards *ʂã* and *ɕia*, we must note that these verbs do not occur as components of SVCs. When they occur immediately after a verb, their pronunciation is *xã* and *xɤ*, respectively, indicating that they are not properly verbs in this context (otherwise they should be pronounced only *ʂã* and *ɕia*). For example:

(75)   箇井里咋水一桶提上了来了。
       kuɤ   tɕĩ=li=tha   ʂui   i   thũ   tshi=xã=lɔ   lɛ=lɔ.
       3   well=LOC=ABL   water one   pail   lift=COMP=PFV come=PFV
       'S/he lifted a pail of water from the well and came.'

(76) 撂下撒！
liɔ=xɤ   sa!
plump=COMP   PART
'Plump it!'

In (75) and (76), one may still find a blurred directional meaning from *xã* and *xɤ* in *tshi=xã* and *liɔ=xɤ*. This is because the content verbs *tshi* 'lift' and *liɔ* 'plump' themselves contain a directional meaning. Note that *xã* and *xɤ* can also follow verbs in no way related to directions, and in this context, they are completely grammaticalized, i.e., their meaning is even more blurred. For example:

(77) 常牧带东沟合并上了。
tʂhãmu   tɛ   tũku   xuɤpĩ=xã=lɔ.
PN   and   PN   merge=COMP=PFV
'The Changmu town and the Donggou town merged.'

(78) 雪下上了着。
ɕyɤ   ɕia=xã=lɔ=tʂɤ.
snow   fall=COMP=PFV=PROG
'The snow was falling.'

(79) 今晚夕扁食捏上。
tɕĩ   uãɕi   piã̰ʂi   niɛ=xã.
today   evening dumpling knead=COMP
'We will knead the dumpling this evening.'

(80) 保证打下了。
potʂḭ̃   ta=xɤ=lɔ.
promise   make=COMP=PFV
'The promise has been made.'

(81) 长假放下了。
tʂhã   tɕia   fã=xɤ=lɔ.
long   vacation give=COMP=PFV
'The long vacation has begun.'

(82) 我啊饿下了。
ŋa   uɤ=xɤ=lɔ.
1:DAT   hungry=COMP=PFV
'I was hungry.'

52 *Verbs and verb phrases*

In these examples, one cannot find any sense related to directionality in the construction V= *xã / xɤ*. This indicates that this construction underwent a complete grammaticalization.

4.5.2 Verb-result constructions

In a verb-result construction, the complement expresses the resultative meaning, or the result of the action of the verb. For example:

(83) 阿吉各家吊死了嘀。
 atɕi   kuɤtɕia   tiɔ=si=lɔ   ti.
 3   self   hang=die=PFV PART
 'S/he hanged her/himself.'

(84) 洋火兰个点着了个。
 iãxuɤ=lã   kɤ   tiã=tʂuɤ=lɔ   kɤ.
 match=INS   this   light=fire=PFV   PART
 'Lit it with the match.'

(85) 个西裤也绊烂了呗？
 kɤ   ɕikhu   iɛ   pã=lã=lɔ   pɨ.
 this   suit_pant   also   stumble=breaking=PFV   PART
 'Was this suit pant also broken as (you) stumbled?'

In (83), the verb *si* is the result of the action denoted by *tiɔ*. In (84), the verb *tʂuɤ* is the result of the action denoted by *tiã*. In (85), the result is expressed by an adjective *lã*, indicating the result of the action denoted by *pã*.

4.5.3 Verb-degree constructions

A verb-degree construction expresses the degree of the action of the verb. Two common structures are used in Zhoutun, namely, V 坏 "V=*xuɛ*" and V 着很/法码 "V=*tʂɤ=xɿ̃/famaˑ*", both of which have an intensifier function. For example:

(86) 扎西连珺啊打着法码。
 tʂaɕi   liãtɕỹ=a   ta=tʂɤ=fama.
 PN   PN=ACC   hit=COMP=hard
 'Zhaxi hit Lianjun hardly.'

(87) 今儿热坏了。
 tɕiɛ   ɻɤ=xuɛ=lɔ.
 today   hot=very=PFV
 'Today is extremely hot.'

(88) a 扎西忙坏了。
     tʂaɕi   mã=xuɛ=lɔ.
     PN   busy=very=PFV
   b 扎西忙着很哩。
     tʂaɕi   mã=tʂʁ=xʁ̃   li.
     PN   busy=COMP=very   PART
     'Zhaxi was very busy.'

(89) a 我啊瞌睡坏了。
     ŋa   khuʐui=xuɛ=lɔ.
     1:DAT   sleepy=very=PFV
   b 我啊瞌睡着很哩。
     ŋa   khuʐui=tʂʁ=xʁ̃   li.
     1:DAT   sleepy=COMP=very   PART
     'I was very sleepy.'

4.6 Valence changing

A productive valence-increasing marker attached to verbs is 给 =ki. ki, used as a verb, means 'give', as in (90).

(90) 我你啊书一本给。
     ŋʁ   nia   fu   i=pʁ̃   ki.
     1   2:DAT   book   one=CL   give
     'I give you a book.'

Added to a verb, =ki is a valence-increasing marker. A construction of the type V=ki has three meanings to be precise: "give", benefactive/malefactive and causative. For example:

(91) 扎西我啊衣裳个买给了。
     tʂaɕi   ŋa   iʂã=kʁ   mɛ=ki=lɔ.
     PN   1:DAT   cloth=CL   buy=VIM=PFV
     'Zhaxi bought me a cloth.'

(92) 再我啊一杯倒给嗒。
     tsɛ   ŋa   i   pi   tɔ=ki   ta.
     again   1:DAT   one   cup   pour=VIM   PART
     'Pour me one more cup of water.'

(93) 伤时贴着的药个取给嗒。
     ʂã   ʂi   thiɛ=tʂʁ=tʁ   yʁ   kʁ   tshu=ki   ta.
     injury   when   paste=PROG=REL   plaster   CL   take=VIM   PART
     'When (someone) gets injured, take a plaster (to somebody).'

(94) 我阿妈哈留给嘀。
ŋɤ   ama=xa   liɯ=kɨ   ti.
1   mother=DAT   leave=VIM   PART
'I left (something) to my mother.'

(95) 嗯你啊书念给的时间没哩。
tɤ   nia   fu   niã=kɨ=tɤ   ʂitɕiã   mɨ   li.
DM   2:DAT   book   read=VIM=REL   time   NEG   PART
'Now I do not have time to read for you.'

(96) 我学生娃的课补给。
ŋɤ   ɕyɤsr̃ua=tɤ   khuɤ   pu=kɨ.
1   students=GEN   lesson   make_up=VIM
'I will make up lessons for the students.'

(97) 补丁补给了。
putĩ   pu=kɨ=lɔ.
fixes   patch=VIM=PFV
'Someone patched for someone else.'

(98) 你阿个门开给了？
ni   akɤ   mɤ̃   khɛ=kɨ=lɔ?
2   who   door   open=VIM=PFV
'You opened the door for whom?'

(99) 脚铐阿吉哈铐给了个。
tɕyɤkhɔ   atɕi=xa   khɔ=kɨ=lɔ   kɤ.
chain   3=DAT   handcuff=VIM=PFV   PART
'Handcuff the chain on him/her.'

(100) 我箇啊没进来给。
ŋɤ   kua   mɨ   tɕĩlɛ=kɨ.
1   3:DAT   NEG   come_in=VIM
'I did not let him/her in.'

(101) 你箇啊一顿饿给嗒。
ni   kua   i=tũ   uɤ=kɨ   ta.
2   3:DAT   one=CL   hungry=VIM   PART
'You starve him/her for a meal.'

(102) 青草一捆捆割，驴哈给掉，吃给。
tɕhɨtshɔ i   khŭkhŭ   kuɤ,   ly=xa   kɨ=tiɔ,   tʂhi=kɨ.
grass   one bundle_bundle   mow   donkey=DAT   give=COMP   eat=VIM
'The grass was mowed bundle by bundle and given to donkeys to eat.'

(103) 个动画片连珺哈笑给了。
 kɤ   tũxuaphiã   liãtey͂=xa   ɕiɔ=ki=lɔ.
 this cartoon   PN=DAT   laugh=VIM=PFV
 'This cartoon made Lianjun laugh.'

In (91), =*ki* increases the valence of the transitive verb *mɛ* 'buy' and the sentence expresses the prototypical event of "giving". The physical "give"-meaning can easily develop into an abstract "give", i.e., the benefactive/malefactive meaning, which literally means "to give benefit/harm to someone". Examples (92)–(94) are transitional examples in which V=*ki* can receive the two readings of physical and abstract "give". In (92), for example, *tɔ=ki* may mean either 'pour to (me)' or 'pour for (me)'. So does *tshuu=ki* in (93). This ambiguity comes not only from the natural linkage between the two types of "give", but also from the head-marking strategy (see Nichols 1986) taken by V=*ki*. In Mandarin Chinese, in contrast, where *gei* 'give' is dependent marking, the two types of "give" can be distinguished through the word order, as in (104).

(104) a 倒一杯水给我。
    dao   yi   bei   shui   gei   wo.
    pour   one   cup   water   gei   1
    'Pour me a cup of water.'
   b 给我倒一杯水。
    gei   wo   dao   yi   bei   shui.
    gei   1   pour   one   cup   water
    'Pour me a water for me.'

In (104a), *wo* is a recipient, while in (104b), *wo* is a beneficiary. In Zhoutun, however, this distinction is not formally made, as there is only V=*ki* at hand.

Examples (95)–(98) demonstrate benefactive meaning of =*ki* in which the new argument of the verb (due to the presence of =*ki*) assumes a beneficiary role. The beneficiary of the action "read" in (95) is "you", and the action "make up lessons" in (96) benefits "students". Note that what can be given to someone is not only beneficial but can also be detrimental. In such a case, the malefactive meaning of =*ki* is expressed, as in (99).

Another common meaning conveyed by the construction V=*ki* is the causative one. In (100), for example, the intransitive verb *tɕĩlɛ* 'come in' becomes transitive with the addition of =*ki*. The meaning of *tɕĩlɛ=ki* is causative or permissive: "allow/let somebody come in". With a transitive verb, such as *tʂhi* 'eat' in (102), =*ki* indicates an additional argument that is not overtly expressed, namely, the agent of *kuɤ* 'mow' and *ki ki* 'give'. The causer in (103), *tũxuaphiã* 'cartoon', an inanimate object, is not supposed to be an argument of *ɕiɔ* 'laugh' without =*ki*.

56 *Verbs and verb phrases*

In some instances, it is not easy to figure out the causer or the causee that directly affects or is affected by the action in the clause with V=*ki*: V=*ki* and V(=*xɤ*) seem to have no difference. For example:

(105) 喟各家的康子兰冰哈捂着消给了着。
 tɤ kuɤtɕia=tɤ khãtsi=lã pĩ=xa u=tʂɤ ɕiɔ=ki=lɔ=tʂɤ.
 DM self=GEN chest=INS ice=ACC cover=PROG thaw=VIM=PFV=PROG
 'He/she himself/herself was covering the ice with his/her chest and the ice has been thawing.'

(106) 奶子哈个里放给了着。
 nɛtsi=xa kɤli fã=ki=lɔ=tʂɤ.
 milk=ACC here put=VIM=PFV=PROG
 'The milk has been put here.'

(107) 网年时下给了着，一个五十米，一个二十米。
 uã niã̠ʂi ɕia=ki=lɔ=tʂɤ, i=kɤ uʂi mi
 net last_year put_down=VIM=PFV=PROG one=CL fifty meter
 i=kɤ ɤʂi mi.
 one=CL twenty meter
 'The nets, one fifty meters and another twenty meters, had been put into the river last year.'

(108) 一晚夕走着，天亮给时还家里不到。
 i uã̠ɕi tsu=tʂɤ, thiã liã=ki ʂi xɛ tɕia=li
 one evening walk=PROG sky light=VIM when still home=LOC
 pu tɔ.
 NEG arrive
 'Someone walked all night and did not arrive home at dawn.'

In (105), the causer of the event *ɕiɔ* 'thaw' is *kuɤtɕia* 'himself/herself', but this causer does not immediately affect the "thawing of ice": there is an interval between the action expressed by *u* 'cover' and the outcome expressed by *ɕiɔ* 'thaw'. Accordingly, it is acceptable to delete =*ki* or replace =*ki* with =*xɤ*. In (106)–(108), it is more acceptable to delete =*ki* or replace it with =*xɤ* because it is hard to figure out what are the arguments of the verbs that are added due to the use of =*ki* in these sentences. Especially in (108), *liã* 'light' is a natural process when the sun rises, and it is hard to say what is its causer.

The following example shows the subtle difference between V=*ki* and V=*xɤ*.

(109) a 电视坏给了，覅动。
 tiã̠si xuɛ=ki=lɔ, pɔ tũ.
 TV break=VIM=PFV NEG:PROHIB move

b 电视坏下了，覅动。
　　tiãsi　　xuɛ=xɤ=lɔ,　　pɔ　　　　　tũ.
　　TV　　　break=COMP=PFV　NEG:PROHIB　move
　　'The TV is broken, and do not touch it.'

Example (109a) indicates that someone or some objective factor (such as a circuit failure) "makes the TV break", while example (109b) does not have this meaning. (109b) merely describes the situation that the TV does not work, without emphasizing that it was someone or some factor that caused this situation.

In some examples, as in (110)–(112), V=*ki* seems to express a passive meaning.

(110) 文鑫娃冻给了。
　　　uɤɕĩ=ua　　tũ=ki=lɔ.
　　　PN=child　　freeze=VIM=PFV
　　　'Wenxin was frozen.'

(111) 人哈迷掉给着嘀。
　　　ɻĩ=xa　　　mi=tiɔ=ki=tʂɤ　　　　　　ti.
　　　people=ACC　bewilder=COMP=VIM=PROG　PART
　　　'People are bewildered.'

(112) 扎西哈狗娃摘给了。
　　　tʂaɕi=xa　　kuua　　　tʂɛ=ki=lɔ.
　　　PN=ACC　　　dog　　　bite=VIM=PFV
　　　'Zhaxi was beaten by a dog.'

The English translations of these examples are all passive. Furthermore, the verb meaning "give" in a range of Chinese dialects is used as a passive marker (Zhou 2016). There is no true passive construction in Zhoutun, however, and =*ki* is therefore not a passive marker. A typical passive construction is a construction in which the valence of the verb decreases, but in Zhoutun =*ki* does not function as a valence-decreasing marker. In (112), for example, *tʂaɕi* (a personal name) and *kuua* 'dog' are the two arguments of the verb *tʂɛ* 'bite', and none of them is deleted or degraded. The "passive" meaning is due to other factors, such as the semantic relation between subject and verb (e.g., a subject with a human referent and the verb "freeze", as in [110]) or the word order (OS instead of SO).

4.7 Possession and existence

The possessive verb and the existential verb are the same verb in Zhoutun: *iu* 'have; exist', with a negative counterpart *mɨ*. For example:

(113) a 扎西街上有哩。
        tʂaɕi   kɛ=xã   iu   li.
        PN   street=LOC   exist   PART
        'Zhaxi is on the street.'
    b 连珺学里有哩。
        liãtɕỹ   ɕyʁ=li   iu   li.
        PN   school=LOC   exist   PART
        'Lianjun is in the school.'

(114) a 阿舅哈钱儿有哩。
        atɕiu=xa   tɕhiɛ   iu   li.
        uncle=DAT   money   exist   PART
        'Uncle has money.'
    b 连珺哈笔三个有哩。
        liãtɕỹ=xa   pi   sã=kʁ   iu   li.
        PN=DAT   pen   three=CL   exist   PART
        'Lianjun has three pens.'

(*iu* in all these examples may be replaced by *mɨ* for expressing an opposite meaning.)

Examples (113) and (114) show that, although the verb *iu* has the same form when used as possessive verb and existential verb, there is a distinction between the form of then possessor and that of the subject of an existential sentence: as shown in (114), the possessor requires the dative marker =*xa*.

Notes

1 In Mandarin Chinese, there are two morphemes *le*. One is added after the verb, as in 我吃了饭 *wo chi le fan* I eat PFV food 'I ate the food.' The second *le* occurs in the final position of a sentence as a final particle that has no meaning for the content.
2 Here "tone" does not refer to "phonemic tone" but "the way a voice sounds".
3 Although in many cases =*li* expresses a future situation, making it perform like a future tense, it is not a tense marker in essence because it can be used in different tense situations: besides the future context, it can also be used in present and even past time, as in 扎西刚房子里去哩 *tʂaɕi tɕiã fãtsi=li tɕhi li* PN a.moment.ago house=LOC go PART 'Zhaxi was going to the house a moment ago.'
4 In Zhoutun, the verb meaning "to have" and "to exist" is *iu*. However, when followed by the particle *kʁ*, the whole expression becomes *iɔ kʁ* instead of *iu kʁ*. It is estimated that *iɔ kʁ* is holistically borrowed from or influenced by Amto Tibetan, which has *jɔ kə* with similar function.

5 Adjectives and adverbs

5.1 Adjectives

5.1.1 Identify adjectives and verbs

The word class of adjectives in Zhoutun is defined on the basis of their syntactic distribution. This section focuses on how adjectives differ from verbs from this point of view.

The distinction between adjectives and verbs should be made clear because they have some features in common. First, both can be used as predicates. For example:

(1) a 今儿热着个。
    tɕiɛ   ȵɣ=tʂɤ=kɣ.
    today   hot=PROG=PART
    'Today is hot.'
  b 扎西面拉着个。
    tʂaɕi   miã   la=tʂɤ=kɣ.
    PN   noodle   pull=PROG=PART
    'Zhaxi is pulling the noodles.'

Second, adjectives and verbs share three types of negation strategies, namely, 不 Adj/V "*pu* Adj/V", Adj/V 着没 "Adj/V=*tʂɤ mi*" and Adj/V 的 *ma re* "Adj/V=*tɣ ma ȵi*". For example:

(2) a 今儿不热。
    tɕiɛ   pu   ȵɣ.
    today   NEG   hot
    'Today is not hot.'

DOI: 10.4324/9781003219361-5

    b   扎西饭不吃。
         tʂaɕi fã   pu   tʂhi.
         PN   meal NEG eat
         'Zhaxi does not eat the meal.'

(3) a   今儿热着没。
         tɕiɛ   ɻʏ=tʂɤ   mi.
         today hot=PROG NEG
         'Today is not hot.'
    b   扎西饭吃着没。
         tʂaɕi fã   tʂhi=tʂɤ mi.
         PN   meal eat=COMP NEG
         'Zhaxi is not eating the meal.'

(4) a   今儿热的 mare。
         tɕiɛ   ɻʏ=tɤ   ma   ɻi.
         today hot=NOMZ NEG   COP
         'Today is not hot.'
    b   扎西饭吃的 ma re。
         tʂaɕi fã   tʂhi=tɤ   ma   ɻi.
         PN   meal eat=NOMZ NEG COP
         'Zhaxi does not eat the meal.'

    It is also possible to distinguish between adjectives and verbs when they occur as predicates.
    First, both adjectives and verbs can be followed by the particles 哩喔 *li uɤ*. The construction "adjective *li uɤ*" expresses, however, a meaning different from the construction "verb *li uɤ*". For example:

(5) a   Adj *li uɤ*:   热哩喔 *ɻʏ li uɤ* 'very hot';   多哩喔 *tuɤ li uɤ* 'very many'...
    b   V *li uɤ*:   喝哩喔 *xuɤ li uɤ* 'drink';   去哩喔 *tɕhi li uɤ* 'go'...

li uɤ in the construction "adjective *li uɤ*" intensifies the adjective, as in *ɻʏ li uɤ*, which means "very hot". But when following a verb, *li uɤ* does not has the same function: in an imperative context, it instead softens the tone of the verb. *Xuɤ li uɤ*, for example, could be uttered by a grandmother when persuading her granddaughter to drink the herbal medicine.

Second, an adjective can be followed by 着很 =tʂɤ=xɤ̃ that enhances the degree of the adjective, while a verb cannot. For example:

(6) 人多着很哩。
    ɭɤ̃   tuɤ=tʂɤ=xɤ̃   li.
    people   many=COMP=very   PART
    'There are too many people.'

Third, both adjectives and verbs can be followed by =xuɛ. However, =xuɛ after an adjective deepens its degree, while after a verb it serves to express the result of the action denoted by the verb. For example,

(7) a 我啊热坏了。
      ŋa   ɭɤ=xuɛ=lɔ.
      1:DAT   hot=xuɛ=PFV
      'I feel too hot.'
   b 手机哈踏坏了。
      ʂutɕi=xa   tha=xuɛ=lɔ.
      mobile_phone=ACC step=xuɛ=PFV
      'The mobile phone was stepped on to be broken.'

Fourth, verbs can be negated by the prohibitive marker 嫑 pɔ, while adjectives cannot. For example:

(8) a 你嫑来！
      ni   pɔ   lɛ!
      2   NEG:PROHIB come
      'Do not come here!'
   b *嫑热！
      pɔ   ɭɤ
      NEG:PROHIB hot

Fifth, only verbs can be followed by 给 =ki. For example:

(9) a 水倒给。
      fɨ   tɔ=ki.
      water   pour=VIM
      'Pour the water (for someone).'
   b *多给。
      tuɤ=ki.
      many=VIM

Lastly, an adjective can directly follow a verb or another adjective. In contrast, when a verb is used after another verb, in most cases 着 *tsɤ* or 了 *lɔ* is needed. For example:

(10) a 个树栽坏了。
  kɤ   fu   tsɛ=xuɛ=lɔ.
  this tree plant=COMP=PFV
  'This tree was badly planted.'
 b 苹果树上跌了下来了。
  phĩkuɤ fu=xã   tiɛ=lɔ   xalɛ=lɔ.
  apple   tree=LOC fall=PFV down=PFV
  'The apple(s) fell down from the tree.'

5.1.2 Adjectives as modifiers

The general rule for adjectives used attributively in Zhoutun is that monosyllabic adjectives are combined directly with nouns, while polysyllabic (mostly disyllabic) adjectives require the addition of attributive marker 的 *tɤ* between the adjective and the noun. This is discussed here.

If an adjective is monosyllabic, it can be combined with the noun directly, especially when the noun is also monosyllabic, and a monosyllabic adjective with a monosyllabic noun generally form a disyllabic phonological word. For example,

(11) 冰水 *pĩ¹¹fɤ⁵⁵*   大路 *ta⁵⁵lu¹¹*   尕娃 *ka¹¹ua¹³*
  'cold water';   'main road';   'little son/kid' . . .

Grammatical disyllabic words without 11 tone (recall the discussion in Section 2.3) can also be formed following the "monosyllabic adjective + monosyllabic noun" scheme. For example:

(12) 红薯 *xũ¹³fu⁵⁵*   公驴 *kũ⁵⁵ly¹³*   暴风 *pɔ⁵⁵fɤ⁵⁵*
  'sweet potato'; 'male donkey'; 'storm wind' . . .

When the adjective is monosyllabic and the noun is disyllabic, the adjective is also combined directly with the noun. For example:

(13) 大阿舅   大丫头   白萝卜
  ta⁵⁵a¹¹tɕiu⁵⁵   *ta⁵⁵ia¹¹thu¹³* ' *pi¹¹luɤ⁵⁵phu¹¹* '
  'the eldest uncle'; 'the first daughter'; 'turnip' . . .

When the adjective is disyllabic, whether the noun is monosyllabic or disyllabic, there is a tendency to add 的 *tɤ* between the adjective and the noun. For example:

(14) 机溜的人 *tɕiliɯ=tɤ ɻĩ* 'smart person'; 好好儿的玩具 *xɔxɤ=tɤ uatɕy* 'good toys'; 粉红的衣裳 *fĩxũ=tɤ iʂã* 'pink clothes' . . .

Zhang (1997) pointed out that the most typical adjectives in Chinese are those that can be freely used as modifiers/attributes. From this perspective, the monosyllabic adjectives are the most typical adjectives in Zhoutun.

5.1.3 *Adjectives as predicates*

When used predicatively (also in comparative constructions), adjectives must be accompanied by certain morphemes, For example:

(15) a ??个人好。
   kɤ ɻĩ   xɔ.
   this person good
   'This person is good.'
 b 个人好哩/着个/着很哩。
   kɤ   ɻĩ   xɔ   li/=tʂɤ kɤ/   =tʂɤ=xɤ̃   li.
   this person good PART/=PROG PART/ =COMP=very PART
   'This person is good/is good/is very good.'

(16) a ??我啊舒坦。
   ŋa   futhã.
   1:DAT comfortable
   'I feel comfortable.'
 b 我啊舒坦哩/着个/着很哩。
   ŋa   futhã   li/ =tʂɤ   kɤ/ =tʂɤ=xɤ̃   li.
   1:DAT comfortable PART/ =COMP   PART/ =COMP=very PART
   'I feel comfortable/feel comfortable/feel very comfortable.'

As can be seen from (15) and (16), regardless of whether monosyllabic or disyllabic, adjectives, when used predicatively, must be followed by components such as *li*, *tʂɤ=kɤ* and *tʂɤ=xɤ̃=li*, otherwise the sentence is awkward.

Here are a few comparative constructions in which the adjective expresses a parameter:

(17) a 扎西我啊高着个。
      tṣaɕi   ŋa   kɔ=tʂʏ   kʏ.
      PN   1:DAT   tall=PROG   PART
      'Zhaxi is taller than me.'
   b 扎西我啊一米高着个。
      tṣaɕi   ŋa   i   mi   kɔ=tʂʏ   kʏ.
      PN   1:DAT   one   meter   tall=COMP   PART
      'Zhaxi is one meter taller than me.'
   c 扎西我啊高着多。
      tṣaɕi   ŋa   kɔ=tʂʏ=tuʏ.
      PN   1:DAT   tall=COMP=much
      'Zhaxi is much taller than me.'

If, in Chinese, it is a common situation that adjectives cannot appear as bare predicates in intransitive sentences, it is a characteristic of Zhoutun that they still cannot appear on their own when they occur as parameters in comparative constructions.

5.2 Adverbs

Adverbs are a heterogeneous word class. As Aikhenvald (2015, 97) claimed, "the concept of 'adverb' is perhaps the most problematic of all word classes". She noted that the typical function of adverbs is to modify verbs but that the concept of "adverb" actually covers a wide range of uses. Adverbs in Zhoutun may be even more "elusive" than this. Unlike in many other languages, they cannot be formed productively by certain morphological means (e.g., the suffix *-ly* in English). In many cases the syntactic function of adverbs (that of modifying verbs) can be realized by nouns, adpositional phrases, etc. This leads to the fact that the adverbs in Zhoutun do not have sufficient morphological and syntactic properties that permit recognizing them, and we can only identify adverbs by combining two criteria: components that can modify verbs and that are not nouns or adpositional phrases are adverbs. Thus, this section discusses adverbs from two perspectives: the position of adverbs and the introduction of some common adverbs.

5.2.1 Position

Despite the fact that adverbs modify verbs, they are not contiguous to verbs. When a verb is transitive and has a noun object, the position of the adverb is before the noun and the verb: "adverb + noun + verb". For example:

(18) a 急赶饭吃！
ɕikã   fã   tʂhi!
hurry meal eat
'Hurry up and eat!'

b 将三天活了嘀。
tɕiã   sã   thiã   xuɣ=lɔ   ti.
only   three day   live=PFV PART
'Someone/something only lived for three days.'

c 你靠酒喝上了呗。
ni   khɔ   tɕiu   xuɣ=xã=lɔ   pɨ.
2   again   wine   drink=COMP=PFV PART
'You have started drinking again.'

If the negative marker 不 *pu* is used, this morpheme occurs immediately before the verb, and its scope includes the preceding adverb. For example:

(19) 你我啊书好好儿不给吗？
ni   ŋa   fu   xɔxɣ   pu   ki   mɣ?
2   1:DAT book in_a_good_manner NEG   give   Q
'Don't you give me (the book) in a good manner?'

When an intransitive verb or a transitive verb without an overt object is modified, the adverb occurs immediately before the verb. For example:

(20) a 你慢慢儿走。
ni   mãmɣ   tsu.
2   slowly   walk
'You walk slowly.'

b 你急赶吃！
ni   tɕikã   tʂhi!
2   hurry   eat
'You hurry up and eat!'

Adverbs also modify adjectives following them. For example:

(21) 安文栋太尕下了。
nãuʐ̃tũ   thɛ   ka=xɣ   lɔ.
PN   too   young=COMP   PART
'Anwendong is too young.'

5.2.2 Some common adverbs

I. *tɕiã* 刚. This adverb, corresponding to 刚 *gang* in Chinese, means "only" and "just". See examples in (22) and (23), which illustrate these two meanings of *tɕiã*.

(22) a 箇刚三天活了嘀。
        kuʐ   tɕiã   sã   thiã   xuʐ=lɔ   ti.
        3   only   three day   live=PFV PART
        'S/he only lived for three days.'
    b 房子里刚三个人有哩。
        fãtsi=li   tɕiã   sã=kʐ   ɹʐ̃   iɯ   li.
        house=LOC only three=CL person exist PART
        'There are only three people in the house.'

(23) a 我刚起来了。
        ŋʐ   tɕiã   tɕhilɛ=lɔ.
        1   just   get_up=PFV
        'I just got up.'
    b 文鑫娃刚学里去了。
        uʐ̃ɕiua   tɕiã   ɕyʐ=li   tɕhi=lɔ.
        PN   just   school=LOC go=PFV
        'Wenxin just went to school.'

II. *tɕikã* 急赶 'hastily' or 'hurry up, without delay'. For example:

(24) 我啊噎下了，急赶背心里捶给哒。
     ŋa   iɛ=xʐ=lɔ,   tɕikã   piɕĩ=li   tʂhui=ki   ta.
     1:DAT choke=COMP=PFV hastily back=LOC pound=VIM PART
     'I choked, hurry and give me a pound on my back.'

III. *ɕiɔthĩ* 消停 'slowly'. For example:

(25) 你消停吃呀喤！
     ni   ɕiɔthĩ   tʂhi   ia   xuã!
     2   slowly   eat   PART   PART
     'You eat slowly!'

IV. *ɹxui* 二回 'again, a second time'. For example:

(26) 你试当，不合适时二回去给呗，合适时你穿呗。
     ni   ʂi   tã,   pu   xuʐʂi   ʂi   ɹxui   tɕhi=ki pi,   xuʐʂi ʂi ni
     2   try   PART NEG fit   if   again go=VIM PART fit   if 2
     tʂhuã   pi.
     wear   PART
     'You try it, if it doesn't fit, send it back again, if it fits, you wear it.'

V. *iliɛ* 一列 'all, completely'. For example"

(27) 碗一列拿上进来，我洗上。
    uã   iliɛ   na=xã   tɕhĩlɛ,   ŋɤ   ɕi=xã.
    bowl all   take=COMP come_in 1   wash=COMP
    'Bring all the bowls in and I'll wash them.'

VI. *imã* 一满 'all, completely'. For example:

(28) 饭一满吃完撒，嫑剩给，浪费着。
    fã   imã   tʂhi=uã   sa,   pɔ   ʂɤ̃=ki,   lãfi=tʂɤ.
    noodle all eat=COMP PART NEG:PROHIB leave=VIM waste=PROG
    'Eat all the noodles! Do not leave them behind! It is a waste.'

The difference between *iliɛ* and *imã* lies in their perspective: *iliɛ* activates a bottom-up perspective, emphasizing the sum of individuals/objects, while *imã* activates the opposite perspective, emphasizing the entire amount of a certain scope.

VII. *xã* 还. It indicates the continuation of a situation ('still') or an increase in a certain degree or an addition to a certain range ('also'). For example:

(29) a 我苹果哈三个吃上了，还吃的心有个。
      ŋɤ phĭkuɤ=xa sã=kɤ   tʂhi=xã=lɔ,   xã   tʂhi=tɤ ɕĩ
      1   apple=ACC three=CL eat=COMP=PFV still eat=REL heart
      iɔ   kɤ.
      have PART
      'I ate three apples and still want to eat.'
    b 嘚我东西买去，还饭做掉嘀。
      tɤ   ŋɤ   tũɕi mɛ tɕhi, xã   fã   tsi=tiɔ   ti.
      DM 1   thing buy go   also meal do=COMP PART
      'I am going to buy something and also cook.'

VIII. *khɔ* 靠 'again'. For example:

(30) a 你靠酒喝上了呗？
      ni   khɔ   tɕiu   xuɤ=xã=lɔ   pi.
      2   again wine drink=COMP=PFV PART
      'You have started drinking again?'

b 高中考不上了着，补习着，补习着靠考不上了。
  kɔtʂũ *khɔ=pu=xã=lɔ=tʂʁ,* *puɕi=tʂʁ,* *puɕi=tʂʁ*
  high_school exam=NEG=COMP= tutorial=PROG tutorial=PROG
       PFV=PROG
  khɔ *khɔ=pu=xã=lɔ.*
  again exam=NEG=COMP=PFV
  'I failed the high school entrance exam, so I took remedial courses. But I did not pass the exam again after the remedial courses.'

5.2.3 Reduplication

Reduplication (often with *r*-ization[1]) is a semi-productive operation that transforms a monosyllabic adjective into an adverb. For example:

(31) a 学生娃我一列好好儿教。
   ɕyʁsʁua *ŋʁ* *iliɛ* *xɔxʁ* *tɕiɔ.*
   student 1 all well teach
   'I will teach all the students carefully.'
  b 你慢慢儿吃。
   ni *mãmʁ* *tʂhi.*
   2 slowly eat
   'Eat slowly.'
  c 雪花尕尕飘着个。
   ɕyʁxua *kaka* *phiɔ=tʂʁ* *kʁ.*
   snowflake little drift=PROG PART
   'Snowflakes are drifting a little.'

In (31), *xɔxʁ* is the reduplicated form of the adjective *xɔ* (with *r*-ization); *mãmʁ* is the reduplicated form of the adjective *mã* (with *r*-ization); and *kaka* is the reduplicated form of the adjective *ka*.

Note

1 Recall Section 2.4 for the discussion on *r*-ization.

6 Minor word classes

6.1 Pronoun

6.1.1 First person

The first-person singular pronoun in Zhoutun is 我 *ŋʏ*, and its plural counterpart is 我们 *ŋʏ=mʏ*. When it is marked by the dative-accusative enclitic =*xa*/=*a*, *ŋʏ* usually becomes 我啊 *ŋa*, while *ŋʏ=mʏ* becomes 我们啊 *ŋʏ=ma*. Some examples containing these forms follow.

(1) a. 我/我们去哩。
   ŋʏ/ ŋʏ=mʏ   tɕhi   li.
   1/ 1=PL   go   PART
   'I am/we are going to leave.'

   b. 我/我们老师 re。
   ŋʏ/ ŋʏ=mʏ   lɔsi   ɖi.
   1/ 1=PL   teacher COP
   'I am a teacher.'

   c. 扎西我啊/我们啊打了。
   tʂaɕi   ŋa/ ŋʏ=ma   ta=lɔ.
   PN   1:ACC/ 1=PL:ACC   hit=PFV
   'Zhaxi hit me/us.'

   d. 扎西我啊/我们啊饭做给。
   tʂaɕi   ŋa/ ŋʏ=ma   fã   tsi=kɨ.
   PN   1:DAT/ 1=PL:DAT   meal   make=VIM
   'Zhaxi made a meal for me/us.'

Note that Zhoutun does not distinguish between the inclusive and exclusive "we/us", unlike Mandarin Chinese, which has exclusive 我们 *women* and inclusive 咱们 *zanmen*.

DOI: 10.4324/9781003219361-6

6.1.2 Second person

The second-person singular pronoun in Zhoutun is 你 *ni*, and its plural counterpart is 你们 *ni=mʏ*. With the dative-accusative enclitic, the two forms turn out to be 你啊 *nia* (2:ACC/DAT) and 你们啊 *ni=ma* (2=PL:ACC/DAT). Examples with these forms can be seen in (1) by replacing the *ŋʏ*-related forms (i.e., *ŋʏ/ ŋʏ=mʏ* and *ŋa/ ŋʏ=ma*) with the *ni*-related forms (i.e., *ni/ ni=mʏ* and *nia/ ni=ma*).

6.1.3 Third person

Zhoutun has two third-person pronouns, namely, 箇 *kuʏ* and 阿吉 *atɕi*. Of the two, *kuʏ* is also a demonstrative meaning "that", as in 箇人 *kuʏ ȵĩ* 'that people, that person', 箇一本书 *kuʏ i=pʏ̃ fu* (that one=CL book) 'that book'. In (2), *kuʏ* is used as a third-person pronoun.

(2) a 箇昨儿来了。
    kuʏ   *tshuʏ*   *lɛ=lɔ.*
    3   yesterday   come=PFV
    'S/he went here yesterday.'
   b 你箇啊打。
    ni   *kua*   *ta.*
    2   3:ACC   beat
    'Beat him/her!'

In (2a), *kuʏ* occurs in subject function with zero marking, while in (2b) it occurs in object function marked by the accusative marker =*xa*/=*a* (*kuʏ*+*a*→*kua*). *kuʏ* can also occur as a genitive element, recipient in ditransitive constructions, etc.

atɕi is another common third-person pronoun, but unlike *kuʏ*, it cannot occur in object function. Therefore, replacing *atɕi* with *kuʏ* in (2b) is impossible. In all other functions, such as genitive, recipient and subject, *atɕi* is free to appear. Another difference between *kuʏ* and *atɕi* is that the former tends to (but not necessarily) refer to the person who is present, while *atɕi* usually refers to the person who is not present.

As regards the origin of third-person pronouns, I hold that *kuʏ* originated from the demonstrative pronoun *kuʏ*, which is likely related to the demonstrative pronoun *kʏ* in Ancient Chinese (also found in some modern Chinese dialects), given that M(andarin) *ʏ* corresponds to *uʏ* in Z(houtun). For example: M *ʏ*: Z *uʏ* 'hungry'; M *xʏ*: Z *xuʏ* 'river; drink'; M *kʏ*: Z *kuʏ* 'cut; brother; song'. As regards *atɕi*, its origin is unclear. Currently, it is speculated that it could be from *tɕia*, the third-person pronoun used in Qiaohua, a local variant of the Xining dialect spoken in Guide County and nearby villages, with the final *a* being dropped and the productive Zhoutun prefix *a-* added.[1] However, further study is needed on this.

6.1.4 Reflexive

In Zhoutun, the reflexive pronoun is 各家 *kuʴtɕia*. It can be used as a core argument (in [3]) or as an emphatic adverbial following a core argument (in [4]).

(3) 箇镜子里咃各家见下了。
    kuʴ   *tɕĩtsi=li=tha*   *kuʴtɕia*   *tɕiã=xʴ=lɔ.*
    3   mirror=LOC=ABL   self   see=COMP=PFV
    'S/he saw her/himself in the mirror.'

(4) 连珺各家学里去哩。
    liãtɕỹ   *kuʴtɕia*   *ɕyʴ=li*   *tɕhi*   *li.*
    PN   self   school=LOC   go   PART
    'Lianjun is going to the school by herself.'

kuʴtɕia is a common reflexive pronoun in Northwest Chinese (Cao 2008).

6.1.5 Locutor-referential

In Zhoutun, there is a special kind of pronoun 咃 *tha* that is not mentioned in the previous literature (to the best of my knowledge). Its function partially overlaps that of a logophoric pronoun (Clements 1975; Culy 1997; Huang 2000). I refer to this pronoun as "locutor-referential pronoun" in the sense that it is a pronoun used to refer to the internal locutor of a clause and/or the narrative locutor of a narration.

Let us begin the discussion on the use of *tha* by listing two examples in which this pronoun might be recognized, at first glance, as an ordinary third-person pronoun.

(5) 扎西来了拿上急赶就走了。咃去哩说。
    tʂaɕi$_i$ *lɛ=lɔ*   *na=xã*   *tɕikã* *tɕiu*   *tsu=lɔ*   *tha$_i$*
    PN   come=PFV take=COMP hurry at_once walk=PFV *tha*
    tɕhi   *li*   *ʂuʴ.*
    go   PART   say
    'Zhaxi$_i$ came. (He$_i$) took (something) and hurried to go. (He$_i$) said that he$_i$ is leaving.'

(6) 安文栋太尕下了，阿吉教着的就初中，小学。青青么假放下时，咄教哩说。
 ãuȓtũ$_i$ thɛ ka=xɤ=lɔ, atɕi$_j$ tɕiɔ=tʂɤ=tɤ tɕiu
 PN too young=COMP=PFV 3 teach=PROG=REL only
 tʂhutʂũ, ɕiɔɕyɤ. tɕhĩtɕhĩ=mɤ$_k$ tɕia fã=xɤ
 junior_middle_school elementary_school PN=PL holiday give=COMP
 ṣi, tha$_j$ tɕiɔ li ṣuɤ.
 when tha teach PART say
 'An Wendong$_i$ is too young. He$_j$ [i.e., a third person] only teaches the students in junior middle school and elementary school. When the students in the age of Qingqing$_k$ began their (winter) vacation, (he$_j$) said that he$_j$ would teach them.' (Context: the speaker tells the addressee that another person, i.e., atɕi 'he', volunteered to teach kids in the village during winter vacation.)

tha in (5) refers to *tʂaɕi* (Zhaxi), the speaker of the utterance "*tɕhi li*". Example (6) involves three participants: *ãuȓtũ* (An Wendong), *atɕi* 'he' and *tɕhĩtɕhĩ* (Qingqing). In this complex context, the pronoun *tha* refers to the participant *atɕi*, i.e., the utterer of the words "*tɕiɔ li*". One may wonder whether *tha* in both examples can be treated as an ordinary third-person pronoun used in the indirect speech context. This is plausible if one considers the context of Mandarin Chinese in which the formally identical *ta* is used in indirect speech while *wo* 'I' is used in direct speech.

(7) a 扎西说他来了。
 Zhaxi shuo ta lai le.
 PN say 3 come PFV
 'Zhaxi said that he came.'
 b 扎西说"我来了"。
 Zhaxi shuo wo lai le.
 PN say 1 come PFV
 'Zhaxi said "I came".'

In the complement clauses of verbs of speech, thought, perception, etc., it is cross-linguistically very common to employ third-person pronouns in indirect reports. I argue, however, that *tha* in (5)–(6) is not ordinarily a third-person pronoun. First, Mandarin *ta*, in indirect speech, can refer to the speaker, but it can also refer to someone else. That is, the referent of Mandarin *ta* is recovered on pragmatic bases rather than on syntax. That is, *ta* in (7a) can refer to a person different from *Zhaxi*. In contrast, it is grammatically established that *tha* in (5)–(6) refers only to *Zhaxi* and *atɕi*, respectively, not to someone else. Second, as discussed later, there are certain contexts in which *tha* cannot be translated 's/he'.

Minor word classes 73

Now, we turn to an intriguing example in which *tha* can literally be translated as "I".

(8) 太小时，咜烧柴拾去时，咜劲不够，背不动呗。
    thɛ   ɕiɔ   ʂi,   tha ʂɔtʂhɛ ʂi tɕhi ʂi, tha
    very young when *tha* firewood pick go when *tha*
    tɕĩ   pu   kɯ,   pɨ=pu=thũ   pɨ.
    strength NEG enough back=NEG=COMP PART
    'When I was very young, every time I went out to pick up firewood, I did not have enough physical strength to shoulder it.'

This example is part of a narration in which the speaker recalls her childhood experience. Here, *tha* refers to the formally unexpressed speaker.

Examples (9)–(10) are two more examples in which *tha* can be interpreted as "I".

(9) 我这么转上了着，过来。玉清丫头咜哈见下了着，急赶箇转过了。
    ŋɤ$_i$ tʂɤmɤ tʂuã=xã=lɔ=tʂɤ,   kɯlɛ. ytɕhĩ$_j$ iathɯ tha$_i$=xa
    1 this turn=COMP=PFV=PROG come PN girl *tha*=ACC
    tɕiã=xɤ=lɔ=tʂɤ, tɕikã kɯ tʂuãkɯ=lɔ.
    see=COMP=PFV=PROG hurry that_way turn=PFV
    'I$_i$ turned this way and went. Yuqing saw me$_i$, and (she) hurried to turn that way.'

In (9), there are two participants, i.e., *ŋɤ* and *ytɕhĩ*. Of the two, *tha* refers to *ŋɤ*, the utterer of the narrative speech. Note that (9) shows that *tha* can function as an object argument marked by the accusative marker =*xa*. In (10), *tha* also refers to "I".

(10) 我黑饭吃上了，没干头，嘚出去了，箇站了。嘚咜站了着，没干头着。
    ŋɤ$_i$ xifã tʂhi=xã=lɔ, mi kãthɯ, tɤ tʂhutɕhi=lɔ,
    1 supper eat=COMP=PFV NEG something_to_do DM go_out=PFV
    kɯ tʂã=lɔ. tɤ tha$_i$ tʂã=lɔ=tʂɤ, mi kãthɯ=tʂɤ.
    there stand=PFV DM *tha* stand=PFV=PROG NEG something_to_do=PROG
    'I$_i$ finished the supper and found nothing to do. Then I$_i$ went out and stood there, having nothing to do.'

Thus far, I have highlighted two contexts in which *tha* refers to "s/he" (as in [5]–[6]) and "I" (as in [8]–[10]). Arguably, *tha* is neither a third-person pronoun nor a first-person pronoun and fundamentally differs from the ordinary third-person pronoun *ta* in Mandarin Chinese.

74 *Minor word classes*

With a closer observation of the two contexts represented by examples (5)–(6) and (8)–(10), one can distinguish two kinds of speakers: the speaker who says something concrete represented the complement clause of a speech verb (e.g., in *John said that he came here yesterday*, the speaker of *he came here yesterday* is *John*); and the speaker of a narration (e.g., in a narration such as *I came here yesterday and met John. I walked along with him. Then I . . .*, the speaker is *I*). For convenience and clarity, henceforth I will avoid the common term "speaker" and use the term "locutor". I will specifically call the first kind of speaker (the one who says something concrete) the "internal locutor" (IL), and the second kind of speaker (the speaker of a narration) the "narrative locutor" (NL). The IL and NL can be the same person, but they do not necessarily need to be. In *I met John yesterday and he said to me that he bought a fantastic book*, for example, the IL of *he bought a fantastic book* is "John" while the NL of the whole narration is "I".

From examples (5)–(6) and (8)–(10), we can conclude that there are two rules connected with the use of *tha*:

(11)   Rules for the use of *tha*:
       Rule 1:   If *tha* occurs in a complement clause of a speech verb, it refers to the IL.
       Rule 2:   If *tha* does not occur in a complement clause of a speech verb, it refers to the NL.

In natural discourse, however, the IL and NL frequently co-occur in the same context. Thus, both Rule 1 and Rule 2 can operate, leading to a situation where *tha*, in the same context, refers to different locutors, as in this example:

(12)   昨儿扎西没去。咃说了，你不去么？
       thsuɤ   tṣaɕi$_i$ mɨ   tɕhi.   tha$_j$ ṣuɤ=lɔ,   ni$_i$ pu   tɕhi   mɤ?
       yesterday PN   NEG   go   tha   say=PFV   2   NEG   go   Q
       tha$_i$ pu   tɕhi.
       tha   NEG   go
       'Zhaxi$_i$ did not go (to some place) yesterday. I$_j$ asked, "Didn't you$_i$ go?" (He$_i$ answered) He$_i$ did not go.'

Here there are two kinds of locutors: the NL "I", which does not overtly appear but is the narrator of the narration, and the IL "Zhaxi", who is the utterer of *pu tɕhi* 'not go'.[2] In this situation, the first *tha*, following Rule 2, refers to the covert NL "I", while the second *tha*, following Rule 1, refers to the internal locutor "Zhaxi".

Note that the two rules of (11) are not obligatory. That is, when a context meets the condition in which *tha* is expected to be used according to (11), *tha* does not necessarily occur. See the following examples:

(13) 1 后头曼阿吉三瓶瓶儿拿上来了，我一个人曼，三瓶瓶儿喝上哩么？
   xuthu   mã   atɕi$_i$ sã   phĩphiɛ   na=xãlɛ=lɔ,   ŋʐ$_j$
   thereafter PART 3   three bottle   take=COMP=PFV   1
   i=kʐ   ɖʐ̃   mã,   sã   phĩphiɛ   xuʐ=xã   li   mʐ?
   one=CL person PART three bottle   drink=COMP PART Q

2 我一斤取上，你我啊一天一斤拿上来，
   ŋʐ$_j$ i=tɕĩ   tshu=xã,   ni$_i$ ŋa$_j$ i   thiã   i=tɕĩ   na=xãlɛ,
   1   one=jin   take=COMP   2   1:DAT   one   day   one=jin   take=COMP

3 阿吉不三不四的我啊骂着，
   atɕi$_i$ pusãpusi=tʐ   ŋa$_j$ ma=tʂʐ,
   3   dirty_words=NOMZ   1:DAT   curse=PROG

   . . . . [an interval with other contents]

4 三斤拿上来了，
   sã=tɕĩ   na=xãlɛ   lɔ,
   three=jin take=COMP   PFV
   咤一个人三斤喝不上啊，
   tha$_j$ i=kʐ   ɖʐ̃   sã=tɕĩ   xuʐ=pu=xã   a,
   LRP   one=CL person three=jin   drink=NEG=COMP   PART

5 咤一斤取，你咤一天一斤拿上来，
   tha$_j$ i=tɕĩ   tshu, ni$_i$,   tha$_j$ i   thiã   i= tɕĩ   na=xãlɛ,
   LRP   one=jin   take   2   LRP   one   day   one=jin   take=COMP

6 阿吉咤哈嘴里不三不四这么的骂着。
   atɕi$_i$ tha$_j$=xa   tsui=li   pusãpusi   tʂʐmʐ=tʐ   ma=tʂʐ.
   3   LRP=DAT   mouth=LOC   dirty_words   this_way=NOMZ   curse=PROG

'[Lines 1–3] Thereafter he$_i$ took three bottles of wine here. I$_j$ am just one person, and (I$_j$) cannot drink up three bottles of wine. (I$_j$ said) "I$_j$ will only take one jin, and you$_i$ take one jin a day to me$_j$." He$_i$ cursed me$_j$ with dirty words . . . [Lines 4–6] (He$_i$ took) three jin (of wine) here. I$_j$ cannot drink up three jin (of wine) alone. (I$_j$ said) "I$_j$ will only take one jin, and you$_i$ take one jin a day to me$_j$." He$_i$ cursed me$_j$ with dirty words.'

Example (13) is an excerpt extracted from a narration. Interestingly, the locutor repeated one sentence after a short interval. The contents in lines 1–3 and 4–6 are basically the same; lines 1 and 4, lines 2 and 5 and lines 3 and 6 are three pairs with similar meanings. One can easily note that the NL *ŋʐ* in line 1, the IL *ŋʐ* in line 2 and the NL *ŋʐ* in line 3 become *tha* in lines 4–6, respectively, showing that the use of *tha* is optional and that ordinary personal pronouns can be used in the same context.

Another example of the non-obligatory use of *tha* is (14).

(14) 1 个奶子不香哩，不要呀，
　　　　kɤ　　nɛtsi　　pu　　ɕiã　　　　　　li,　　pu　　iɔ　　　ia,
　　　　this　milk　NEG　taste_sweet　PART　NEG　want　PART
　　　　阿奶个奶子啊不要。
　　　　anɛ　　　　　kɤ　　nɛtsi=a　　pu　　iɔ.
　　　　grandmother　this　milk=ACC　NEG　want

2 嗯个啊撂下了。
　　tɤ　　ka　　　　liɔ=xɤ=lɔ.
　　DM　this:ACC　put_down=COMP=PFV

3 坨哈奶不爱啊，扎西你咂上。
　　thaᵢ=xa　　nɛ　　　pu　　nɛ　　a,　　tʂaɕi　ni　tsa=xã.
　　LRP=DAT　milk　NEG　like　PART　PN　　2　　suck=COMP

4 阿吉个啊咂惯了着，不要哩。
　　atɕiⱼ　ka　　　　　tsa=kuã=lɔ=tʂɤ,　　　　pu　　iɔ　　li.
　　3　　this:ACC　suck=habituate=PFV=PROG　NEG　want　PART

5 开水点儿掺给时，给掉时，
　　khɛʂui　tie　　tshã=ki　　ʂi,　　ki=tiɔ　　　ʂi,
　　water　little　mix=VIM　COND　give=COMP　COND

6 我不咂，奶奶香着没哩。
　　ŋɤᵢ　　pu　　tsa,　　nɛnɛ　　ɕiã=tʂɤ　　　　　　mi　　li.
　　1　　NEG　suck　milk　taste_sweet=PROG　NEG　PART

'"The milk does not taste good; (Iᵢ) do not want it. (Ii) do not want the milk." And (sheᵢ) put the milk down. (Sheᵢ said) Sheᵢ does not like the milk. Zhaxiⱼ, youⱼ drink it. Sheᵢ is used to drinking the (pure) milk and does not want the one with water. Even if only a little water is mixed into the milk and given (to her), (sheᵢ would say) "Iᵢ will not drink it, the milk does not taste good."'

The locutor of (14) is a grandmother who is talking (to her friend) about her granddaughter: her little granddaughter does not drink milk mixed with water. In line 3, *tha*, according to Rule 1, is used to refer to the granddaughter, the IL, with the speech verb being omitted. However, in line 6, although based on Rule 1, the IL (the granddaughter) could be referred to by *tha*, the first-person pronoun *ŋɤ* is used instead.

From the previous description, it can be concluded that *tha* is not prominent in Zhoutun. First, *tha* is used only in a particular context, i.e., in natural discourse. It never occurs in the data collected through elicitation (at least in those collected during my fieldwork),³ which shows that native speakers do not consider *tha* to be a commonly used pronoun in the grammar system and that they perceive *tha* as having no importance because in those contexts of natural discourse where *tha* occurs, they use ordinary personal pronouns instead in elicitation queries. Second, even in natural discourse, the use of *tha* is not mandatory. Ordinary personal pronouns can be used in the position where *tha* could be used.

6.2 Demonstratives

6.2.1 *The system*

The basic demonstratives in Zhoutun are the proximal one 个 *kɤ* and the distal one 箇 *kuɤ*. These two demonstratives constitute a simple two-term system. Both of these elements can be used as arguments or as modifiers.

In addition to these two demonstratives, there is a demonstrative morpheme 兀 *u* that can be combined with *kɤ* and *kuɤ* to form 兀个 *u=kɤ* and 兀箇 *u=kuɤ*, respectively, indicating a distance longer than what *kɤ* and *kuɤ* refer to. The duration of *u* can be lengthened iconically. For example, *u:=kɤ* refers to a location that has a longer distance than *u=kɤ* does, and *u::=kɤ* refers to a location that has even longer distance.

6.2.2 *Animate and inanimate referents*

kɤ and *kuɤ* are used to refer to animate and inanimate referents, either as arguments (15) or modifiers (16).

(15) a 个坏下了，箇坏着没。
  kɤ   xuɛ=xɤ=lɔ,   kuɤ   xuɛ=tʂɤ   mi.
  this broken=COMP=PFV that broken=PROG NEG
  'This is broken, that is not broken.'
 b 个/箇扎西 mare，个/箇连珺 re。
  kɤ/ kuɤ   tʂaɛi ma   ȵi,   kɤ/ kuɤ   liãtɕỹ   ȵi.
  this/that PN   NEG COP   this/that PN   COP
  'This/that is not Zhaxi, this/that is Lianjun.'
 c 你个啊吃么箇啊吃？
  ni ka   tʂhi mɤ   kua   tʂhi?
  2   this:ACC eat   DISJ that:ACC eat
  'You eat this or that?'
 d 你我啊个/箇给撒。
  ni ŋa   kɤ/ kuɤ   ki   sa.
  2   1:DAT this/that give PART
  'You give me this/that.'

78 Minor word classes

In the previous examples, *kɤ/kuɤ* is used in subject function (15a)–(15b) and in object function (15c)–(15d).

(16) a 箇们箇面饭吃着嘀。
    kuɤ=mɤ kuɤ=miã fã   tʂhi=tʂɤ ti.
    3=PL   that=side meal eat=PROG PART
    'They are eating over there.'

b 个娃孽障喜着很哩！
    kɤ   ua   niɛtʂã ɕi=tʂɤ=xɤ̃   li!
    this child pity   like=COMP=very PART
    'This child is so adorable!'

c 你们个几个里阿个啊饿下了？
    ni=mɤ kɤ   tɕi=kɤ=li   aka   uɤ=xɤ=lɔ?
    2=PL   this several=CL=LOC   who:DAT   hungry=COMP=PFV?
    'Which one of you is hungry?'

d 郭*（一）个人啊我没见。
    kuɤ   *(i)=kɤ   ʅɤ̃   a   ŋɤ   mɨ   tɕiã.
    that one=CL   person   ACC 1   NEG see
    'I did not see that person.'

e 郭人郭死上了三年了嘀。
    kuɤ   ʅɤ̃   kuɤ   si=xã=lɔ   sã   niã   ti.
    that person that   die=COMP=PFV   three year PART
    'That person has been dead for three years.'

f 个门个开着个。
    kɤ   mɤ̃   khɛ=tʂɤ   kɤ.
    this door open=PROG   PART
    'This door is open.'

g 个事情个顺当着很哩。
    kɤ   sitɕhĩ kɤ   ʂũtã=tʂɤ=xɤ̃   li.
    this thing   this smooth=COMP=very PART
    'This thing went very well.'

h 郭人郭啊饿了。
    kuɤ   ʅɤ̃   kua   uɤ=lɔ.
    that person 3:DAT hungry=PFV
    'That person was hungry.'

Example (16a) shows the use of *kuɤ* as a personal pronoun (*kuɤ=mɤ* 'they') and a demonstrative adjective (*kuɤ miã* 'that side'). Example (16b) illustrates that *kɤ* can also be used as a demonstrative modifier. Example (16c) shows that if the noun is modified by *kɤ* (or *kuɤ*) and a numeral (with a classifier), the order is "demonstrative + numeral-CL + noun". Note that numerals in Zhoutun often occur after the head noun (e.g., 人一个 *ʅɤ̃ i=kɤ* (person one=CL) 'one person'), but when a demonstrative is added, the order is "demonstrative + numeral-CL + noun"; see Zhou (2020b) for detail. Example (16d) indicates that when the numeral is *i* 'one', the numeral cannot be omitted. In other words, the expression *个/簡个人 *kʁ/kuʁ=kʁ ɻĩ (this/that CL person) 'this/that person' is not allowed and must be reformulated as 个/簡一个人 *kʁ/kuʁ i=kʁ ɻĩ* 'this/that one person'. This construction is different from a noun phrase that does not contain a demonstrative. In the "noun+numeral-CL" phrase of Zhoutun, if the numeral is 'one', it can be omitted, as in 人个来了 *ɻĩ=kʁ lɛ=lɔ* (person=CL come=PFV) 'A person came'.

Examples (16e)–(16g) show a special use of the demonstrative in a "demonstrative + noun + demonstrative" construction. In this example, the two demonstratives are identical, and the second is used to refer to the whole "demonstrative + noun" noun phrase before it. This construction does not seem to differ semantically from the simple sequence "demonstrative + noun". In fact, the second demonstrative of a "demonstrative + noun + demonstrative" construction can be freely omitted. However, the "demonstrative + noun + demonstrative" structure has some characteristics of its own. First, the noun in this construction is a bare noun, and no other components, such as adjectives, can modify it, which means the component occurring between the two demonstratives must be as short as possible. Second, the construction can only be used in subject function (and not, for example, in object function). Third, even though the second demonstrative can be omitted freely, the first cannot, thus a construction "noun + demonstrative" is unacceptable. Finally, as shown in example (16h), when the construction "demonstrative + noun + demonstrative" semantically indicates an experiencer, the dative marker is added to the second demonstrative.

6.2.3 Location referents

kʁ and *kuʁ* cannot refer to locations by their own unless certain formal changes are made. First, *r*-ization is necessary. Although the vowels in *kʁ* and *kuʁ* remain unchanged under *r*-ization, the tone reflects a change: $kʁ^{55}/kuʁ^{55}$ (*r*-ization) > $kʁ^{13}/kuʁ^{13}$, written 个儿/簡儿. For example:

(17) a 个儿坐。
      kʁ   tsuʁ.
      here sit
      'Sit here.'
   b 扎西簡儿有哩。
      tʂaɕi kuʁ iu li.
      PN   there exist PART
      'Zhaxi is there.'

Beyond its basic function of referring to a distant location, *kuʀ* can also be used as an interjection, as illustrated by the following example:

(18) 箇儿！箇儿！箇儿！
    kuʀ!   *kuʀ!*   *kuʀ!*
    that   that   that

A typical context for (18) is when a parent instructs a child to be careful about something, such as not spilling food everywhere at dinner, but the child accidentally spills the food on the table or knocks the bowl to the floor. The parent would say (18), meaning "Look! Look! Look! I've told you not to do that, but you still do it", with a tone of blame in this case. In other cases, such a blaming tone may not appear and the interjection *kuʀ* simply means "Look!". For example, if the speaker expects a certain person to appear on the TV news and the moment the speaker saw the person on the TV news, the speaker can say (18). *kuʀ* appears at least once and can be repeated up to three or four times. The number of repetitions is proportional to the strength of the feelings expressed. In short, the interjection *kuʀ* is used for expressing "something you expected or worried about happened", indicating the speaker's blame, or "see, I'm right!".

kʀ/kuʀ can also form, with the locative 里 *li*, the construction 个/箇里 *kʀ/kuʀ=li* and, with 面 *miã*, the construction 个/箇面 *kʀ/kuʀ=miã*. Both constructions refer to locations. For example:

(19) a 扎西个里有哩。
      tṣaɕi   *kʀ=li*   *iɯ*   *li.*
      PN   this=LOC   exist   PART
      'Zhaxi is here.'
   b 你们个儿坐，郭们箇面坐。
      ni=mʀ   *kʀ*   *tsuʀ,*   *kuʀ=mʀ*   *kuʀ=miã*   *tsuʀ.*
      2=PL   here   sit   3=PL   that=side   sit
      'You sit here, they sit there.'

There are, however, subtle differences between *kʀ/kuʀ=li* and *kʀ/kuʀ=miã*. In general terms, the former refers to a specific place, while the latter refers to a generic location. For example, when answering the question "Do you have bananas here?", one can use both *kʀ=li* or *kʀ=miã*: with *kʀ=li* one refers to a specific place (e.g., every house here has bananas), while *kʀ=miã* one refers to a broader location (e.g., bananas exist in this area).

6.2.4 Manner and degree

When referring to manner and degree, Zhoutun uses another set of words, i.e., 这么 *tsʏmʏ* and 那么 *namʏ*, instead of *kʏ*, *kuʏ* and their related forms. When referring to manner, *tsʏmʏ* and *namʏ* function as a noun (as in [20]), and when referring to degree, they precede adjectives (as in [21]). For example:

(20) a re 么这么说着嗒？
  .ɨ mʏ tsʏmʏ ʂuʏ=tʂʏ ta?
  COP Q this_way say=PROG PART
  'Is it right to say that?'
  b 你话那么说时，亲戚高兴的 mare 喔。
  ni xua namʏ ʂuʏ ʂi, tɕhĩtɕhi
  2 word that_way say when guest
  kɔɕĩ=tʏ ma .ɨ uʏ.
  happy=NOMZ NEG COP PART
  'When you said like that, the guests were not happy.'

(21) a 你般这么高的草摞着哩。
  ni=pã tsʏmʏ kɔ=tʏ tshɔ luʏ=tʂʏ li.
  2=POST this_way tall=NOMZ grass stack=PROG PART
  'There are stacks of grass as tall as you are.'
  b 个娃这么大哩么那么大哩？
  kʏ ua tsʏmʏ ta li mʏ namʏ ta li?
  this child this_way tall PART DISJ that_way tall PART
  'Is this child this tall or that tall?'

6.3 Interrogative words

6.3.1 tuʏ- words

In Zhoutun, there are two *wh*- words beginning in 多 *tuʏ*-, namely, 多少 *tuʏʂɔ* and 多早 *tuʏtsɔ*. The former is used to inquire about quantity, including the number of things, prices, and ages of people, and can be translated as 'how many', 'how much' or 'how old' depending on the situation; the latter is used to inquire about time, i.e., 'when'. For example:

(22) a 你多少了？
  ni tuʏʂɔ=lɔ?
  2 how_old=PFV
  'How old are you?'

b 个多少？
    kɤ   tuɻʂɔ?
    this how_much
    'How much is it?'
c 个列多少有个？
    kɤ=liɛ   tuɻʂɔ   iɔ   kɤ?
    this=PL   how_many   have   PART
    'How many of these are there?'

(23) a 你多早来哩？
    ni   tuɻtsɔ   lɛ   li?
    2   when   come   PART
    'When will you come?'
b 多早的车？
    tuɻtsɔ=tɤ   tʂhɤ?
    when=NOMZ   bus
    'When do you take the bus tomorrow?'

6.3.2 *a- words*

Another two Zhoutun *wh-* words begin in *a-*: 阿里 *ali* 'where' and 阿个 *akɤ* 'who; what'. For example:

(24) a 你阿里咃来了？
    ni   ali=tha   lɛ=lɔ?
    2   where=ABL   come=PFV
    'Where did you come from?'
b 全息你阿里睡了？
    tɕhyã̄ɕi   ni   ali   ʂui=lɔ?
    last_night   2   where   sleep=PFV
    'Where did you sleep last night?'
c 箇人阿里的 re？
    kuɤ   ɻĩ   ali=tɤ   ɻi?
    that   person   where=NOMZ   COP
    'Where is that person from?'

If the predicate of the clause is 去 *tɕhi* 'go', the final syllable of *ali* could be omitted. For example:

(25) 扎西阿去了？
    tʂaɕi   a   tɕhi=lɔ?
    PN   where   go=PFV
    'Where is Zhaxi?'

Next are examples of *akʏ*. It refers to a person in (26) and an object in (27).

(26) a 你们个几个里阿个啊饿下了？
   ni=mʏ   kʏ   tɕi=kʏ=li   akʏ=a   uʏ=xʏ=lɔ?
   2=PL   this several=CL=LOC   who=DAT hungry=COMP=PFV
   'Which one of you is hungry?'

   b 箇阿个 re？
   kuʏ   akʏ   ʥi?
   that   who   COP
   'Who is that?'

   c 阿个的帽子破下了？
   akʏ=tʏ   mɔtsi   phʏ=xʏ=lɔ?
   who=GEN   hat   break=COMP=PFV
   'Whose hat was broken?'

   d 早晨阿个来时你水倒给。
   tsɔsʏ̃   akʏ   lɛ   ʂi   ni   ʂuɨ   tɔ=kɨ.
   tomorrow   who   come   when   2   water pour=VIM
   'You pour water for whoever comes tomorrow.'

(27) a 你阿个拿上？
   ni   akʏ   na=xã?
   2   which   take=COMP
   'Which one do you take?'

   b 你阿个一本书啊看着哩？
   ni   akʏ   i=pʏ̃   fu=a   khã=tʂʏ   li?
   2   which   one=CL   book=ACC   read=PROG   PART
   'Which book are you reading?'

6.3.3 -mʏ words

There are also two *wh-* words that have in common the final syllable *mʏ*: *ʂʏ̃mʏ* 'what' and *tʂima* 'how'. *ʂʏ̃mʏ* is used mainly to refer to concrete inanimate referents (28a)–(28d) and actions (28e)–(28f). For example:

(28) a 个什么 re？
   kʏ   ʂʏ̃mʏ   ʥi?
   this what   COP
   'What is this?'

   b 你啊什么吃的心有个？
   nia   ʂʏ̃mʏ   tʂhi=tʏ   ɕĩ   iɔ   kʏ?
   2:DAT   what   eat=REL   heart   have   PART
   'What do you want to eat?'

c 个什么杯子 re?
kʏ ʂɤ̃mʏ pitsi ɖi?
this what cup COP
'What kind of material is this cup?'

d 什么兰做下的 re?
ʂɤ̃mʏ=lã tsi=xʏ=tʏ ɖi?
what=INS make=COMP=REL COP
'What is this made of?'

e 扎西什么做着个?
tʂɕi ʂɤ̃mʏ tsi=tʂʏ kʏ?
PN what do=PROG PART
'What is Zhaxi doing?'

f 你早晨羊荡去哩么什么做去哩?
ni tsɔʂɤ̃ iã tã tɕhi li mʏ ʂɤ̃mʏ tsi tɕhi li?
2 tomorrow sheep herd go PART DISJ what do go PART
'Are you going to herd sheep tomorrow or are you going to do something else?'

tʂima is used to ask about manner (29a)–(29b) and status (29c)–(29d). For example:

(29) a 我你啊怎么说了!
ŋʏ nia tʂima ʂuʏ=lɔ!
1 2:DAT how say=PFV
'How I told you!'

b 怎么跳了嘀?
tʂima thiɔ=lɔ ti?
how jump=PFV PART
'How did (you) jump?'

c 你个两天论文怎么写着个?
ni kʏ liã thiã lũuʏ̃ tʂima ɕiɛ=tʂʏ kʏ?
2 this two day paper how write=PROG PART
'How did you do on your paper in the last two days?'

d 个儿咜西宁怎么有哩?
kʏ=tha ɕinĩ tʂima iu li?
here=ABL Xining how have PART
'How far is it from here to Xining?'

6.3.4 Others

There are two atypical interrogative words in Zhoutun in the sense that they do not always express interrogative meaning. They are 几 *tɕi* and 来 *lɛ*.

In declarative clauses, *tɕi* refers to an indefinite quantity ('several'). For example:

(30) 几辆车停着个。
    tɕi=liã   *tʂhɤ*   *thĩ=tʂɤ*   *kɤ.*
    several=CL   car   park=PROG   PART
    'Several cars parked there.'

In interrogative clauses, *tɕi* is used to ask for a quantity when the subjective expectations are that of a small quantity. For example:

(31) a 早晨几个人来哩？
    tsɔʂɤ   *tɕi=kɤ*   *ɻĩ*   *lɛ*   *li?*
    tomorrow   several=CL   person   come   PART
    'How many people are coming tomorrow?'
    b 板凳儿几个有哩？桌子几个有哩？
    pãtɤ   *tɕi=kɤ*   *iu*   *li?*   *tʂuɻtsi*   *tɕi=kɤ*   *iu*   *li?*
    bench   several=CL   exist   PART   table   several=CL   exist   PART
    'How many benches and tables are there?'

Note that the interrogative reading in (31) is not exclusively represented by *tɕi*. The rising tone of the sentence also contributes to the interrogative interpretation. Without the rising tone, the two sentences can be declarative sentences, expressing "several people are coming tomorrow" and "there are several benches and tables", respectively, just like (30) where no rising tone is presented. But, on the other hand, without *tɕi*, even in the presence of a rising tone, these two sentences cannot be the *wh-* questions[4]. So, it can be claimed that *tɕi* (partially) participates in the formation of a *wh-* question.

The interrogative word 来 *lɛ* occurs in sentence-final position after a noun. The sequence "noun *lɛ*" is used to ask about the location of the referent of the noun. For example:

(32) a 扎西来？
    tʂaɕi   *lɛ?*
    PN   PART
    'Where is Zhaxi?'
    b 箇一本书来？
    kuɤ   *i=pɤ̃*   *fu*   *lɛ?*
    that   one=CL   book   PART
    'Where is that book?'

86 *Minor word classes*

The particularity of *lɛ* is that it cannot constitute a question by itself. It is always a construction "noun *lɛ*" that expresses the question. In addition, *lɛ* cannot be omitted, so, for example, the sole *tṣaɕi* cannot constitute a question asking for the location of *tṣaɕi* (Zhaxi). Therefore, *lɛ* can be considered as an obligatory component that in the "N *lɛ*" construction.

6.4 Numerals

6.4.1 Cardinal and ordinal numerals

Cardinal numerals comprise the coefficient numerals and the digit numerals, all of which are derived from Chinese. For example:

(33) a coefficient numerals: *lĩ* 零 'zero', *i* 一 'one', *ɤ* 二 'two', *sã* 三 'three', *si* 四 'four', *u* 五 'five', *liu* 六 'six', *tɕhi* 七 'seven', *pa* 八 'eight', *tɕiu* 九 'nine', *ʂi* 十 'ten'.
  b digit numerals: *ʂi* 十 'ten'⁵、*pɨ* 百'hundred'、*tɕhiã* 千 'thousand'、*uã* 万 'ten thousands'.

The combination of a coefficient numeral and a digit numeral is used to express numbers above ten. In 一百二十三 'one hundred and twenty-three', for example, 'one', 'two' and 'three' are coefficient numerals, and 'hundred' and 'ten' are digit numerals.

In Zhoutun, the most productive way to form an ordinal numeral is to add the prefix 第 to a cardinal numeral. For example,

(34) *tsi-i* 第一 'first', *tsi-ɤ* 第二 'second', *tsi-sãʂi-ɤ* 第三十二 'thirty-second'

6.4.2 Fractional numerals

There are two common ways to express fractional numerals in Zhoutun.

i "coefficient numeral + classifier + coefficient numeral". The classifier varies depending on the object, such as 五块二 *u khuɛ ɤ* 'five yuan two; 5.2 yuan', 六米一 *liu meter i* '6.1 meters', etc. Another way for expressing decimals is through the expression "coefficient word + *tiã* 'point' + coefficient word" (such as "four point three"), but this is rarely used in everyday speech.

ii "coefficient word + 成 *tʂhɤ̃* / 折 *tʂɤ*". This expression is equivalent to "coefficient numeral-tenths", for example, *sã tʂhɤ̃/ tʂɤ* means "three-tenths". The expression "十分之 *ʂi fɤ̃ tsi* ten fraction of + coefficient numeral" can also be used but is rarely used in practice. For example, *ʂi fɤ̃ tsi sã* means "three-tenths".

6.5 Classifiers

6.5.1 Nominal classifiers

Nominal classifiers can be divided into measurable and non-measurable. The measurable classifiers are related to length, weight and measurement. In Zhoutun, they are essentially the same forms used in Mandarin Chinese, including 斤 *tɕĩ* 'jin',[6] 米 *mi* 'meter', 亩 *mu* 'mu',[7] etc. The non-measurable classifiers can be divided into individual classifiers, collective classifiers and indefinite classifiers according to the noun attributes they modify, and into specialized classifiers and temporary classifiers according to whether they are used exclusively as classifiers or not. Table 6.1 lists a number of common nominal classifiers in Zhoutun.

Nominal classifiers in Zhoutun are mostly monosyllabic and are subject to *r*-ization, reduplication, or both. Although the specialized classifiers are fewer than the temporary classifiers, in terms of token frequency, the specialized classifier 个 *kɤ* is used far more frequently than any other. There are so many nouns that can be used with *kɤ* in Zhoutun, including, but not limited to, the following.

(35) 被/笔 / 虫儿 /门/灯 / 地方/飞机/佛 / 马/毛巾/帽子/铺子/枪 / 桥/树 / 椅子/猪/ 桌子 . . . . . .
pi/pi/tɕhyɤ/mɤ̃/tɤ̃/tsifã/fitɕi/fɤ/ma/mɔtɕĩ/mɔtsi/phutsi/tɕhiã/tɕhiɔ/fu/itsi/tʂu/tʂuɤtsi . . .
'quilt/pen/worm/door/lamp/place/plane/Buddha statue/horse/towel/hat/store/gun/tree/chair/pig/table . . .'

The same nouns occur with other classifiers in Mandarin Chinese.

Table 6.1 Some nominal classifiers in Zhoutun

Classifiers	Attributes of the classifier
瓣 *pã*	individual; temporary
班 *pã*	collective; specialized
帮 *pã*	collective; specialized
包 *pɔ*	collective; temporary
杯 *pi*	individual; temporary
篮篮儿 *lãlɤ*	collective; temporary
滴儿 *tiɛ*	individual; specialized
提提 *tshitshi*	collective; temporary

6.5.2 Verbal classifiers

Verbal classifiers in Zhoutun include 次 *tshi*, 回 *xui*, 遍 *piã*, 锤 *tʂhui*, 个 *kʅ* and other forms. The verb classifier phrase has the structure "cardinal numeral + verbal classifier" and occurs before the verb. The cardinal numeral cannot be omitted even if it is 'one'.

Among the verbal classifiers, *kʅ* is again the most frequently used. For example:

(35) a 牙一个刷。
         ia   i=kʅ   ʂua.
         tooth   one=CL   brush
         'To brush teeth.'

     b 你一个拾掇给哒。
         ni   i=kʅ   ʂituʅ   ta.
         2   one=CL   tidy   PART
         'You clean it up.'

In (35a), *i=kʅ* appears before the verb 'brush'. Note that since it also occurs after the noun 'tooth' and the typical position for a nominal classifier phrase (NCP) is after the noun it modifies, i.e., "noun + NCP" (see Section 6.5.3), *i=kʅ* could be analyzed as an NCP in (35a). However, this *i=kʅ* is a verbal classifier phrase rather than a nominal one, as its meaning and form reveal. First, semantically, *i=kʅ* does not refer to the number of the referents of the noun *ia* as *i* 'one' (you do not brush just one tooth); a similar case can be found in 手一个洗 *ʂu i=kʅ ɕi* hand one=CL wash 'to wash hands'. Second, as mentioned earlier, when the cardinal numeral in a nominal classifier phrase is "one", it can be omitted (e.g., 苹果个拿上 *phĩkuʅ kʅ na=xã* apple=CL take=COMP 'to take an apple'). However, *i* 'one' in (35a) cannot be omitted. In (35b), *i=kʅ* is used to modify the verb "to clean up" and does not modify the pronoun "you".

6.5.3 The position of Num+CL and noun

In Zhoutun, an NCP can either follow or precede the noun it modifies, forming the structures "noun + NCP" and "NCP + noun", respectively. Of the two structures, the former is used far more frequently than the latter, especially when the noun does not occur in subject function. The structure "NCP + noun" is used under three particular circumstances.

First, if the numeral is emphasized, the NCP usually precedes the noun. See Example (36).

Minor word classes 89

(36) 我三个苹果吃了，再不吃了。
    ŋɤ   sã=kɤ   phĩkuɤ   tʂhi=lɔ,   tsɛ   pu   tʂhi=lɔ.
    1   three=CL   apple   eat=PFV,   again   NEG   eat=PFV
    'I have eaten three apples and am not eating any more.'

In example (36), the speaker emphasizes that (s)he has eaten THREE apples and thus cannot or does not want to eat any more. Under this circumstance, the construction "NCP + noun" can be used.

The second circumstance under which the NCP precedes the noun is when a demonstrative is added. See example (37).

(37) a   我个三个苹果吃了。
        ŋɤ   kɤ   sã=kɤ   phĩkuɤ   tʂhi=lɔ.
        1   this   three=CL   apple   eat=PFV
   b   *我苹果个三个吃了。
        ŋɤ   phĩkuɤ   kɤ   sã=kɤ   tʂhi=lɔ.
        1   apple   this   three=CL   eat=PFV
   c   *我个苹果三个吃了。
        ŋɤ   kɤ   phĩkuɤ   sã=kɤ   tʂhi=lɔ.
        1   this   apple   three=CL   eat=PFV
        'I ate these three apples.'

Example (37) indicates that when a demonstrative is added, the only possible structure is "demonstrative + NCP + noun", while the NCP cannot be placed after the noun.

Last, if the noun that is modified by the NCP is relativized, the NCP should precede it. See example (38).

(38) a   我扎西哈书一本给掉了。
        ŋɤ   tʂaɕi   xa   fu   i=pɤ̃   ki=tiɔ=lɔ.
        1   PN   DAT   book   one=CL   give=COMP=PFV
        'I gave Zhaxi a book.'
→ b   我扎西哈给掉的（箇）一本书
        ŋɤ   tʂaɕi   xa   ki=tiɔ=tɤ   (kuɤ)   i=pɤ̃   fu
        1   PN   DAT   give=COMP=REL   that   one=CL   book
        'The book I gave to Zhaxi'

Unlike the NCP, the only position of the verb classifier phrase is before the verb. Hence, Example (39) is ungrammatical.

(39) *我北京去了三回。
 *ŋɤ　　*pitɕĩ*　　　*tɕhi=lɔ*　　*sã=xuɨ*.
 1　　　Beijing　　go=PFV　　three=CL
 'I went to Beijing three times.'

In summary, the NCP in Zhoutun follows the noun in most cases and precedes it when (i) the numeral is emphasized, (ii) accompanied by a demonstrative or (iii) the noun it modifies is relativized. On the other hand, the verb classifier phrase only precedes the verb; see Zhou (2020b) for details.

6.6 Final particles

Final particles are a distinctive class of words in Chinese generally used to express the tone of the clause. Final particles do not contribute to the truth-value semantics, but they tend to reflect the subjective attitude and perception of the speaker. For example, some particles are used in interrogative sentences and can be called interrogative particles. The core function of a particular final particle is, however, difficult to generalize, either because its semantics is elusive or because it can be used in different kinds of sentences and it expresses different meanings.

Here I list ten common final particles of Zhoutun.

6.6.1 ti

ti 嘀 is primarily used in declarative sentences to express a high degree of certainty as to what is being said or to emphasize that what is being said. For example:

(40) a 个狗娃二十年活了嘀。
　　　 kɤ　　*kuua*　　*ɤʂi*　　*niã*　　*xuɤ=lɔ*　　*ti*.
　　　 this　 dog　　　twenty　year　　live=PFV　　PART
　　　 'The dog lived for ten years.'
　　b 昨儿扎西麻雀一个打了嘀。
　　　 tshuɤ　　*tʂaɕi*　　*matɕhyɤ*　　*i=kɤ*　　*ta=lɔ*　　*ti*.
　　　 yesterday　PN　　　sparrow　　　one=CL　　shoot=PFV　PART
　　　 'Yesterday Zhaxi shot a sparrow.'
　　c 我们等着等着，天亮下了嘀。
　　　 ŋɤ=mɤ　　*tɤ̃=tʂɤ*　　*tɤ̃=tʂɤ*,　　*thiã*　　*liã=xɤ=lɔ*　　*ti*.
　　　 1=PL　　　wait=PROG　wait=PROG　sky　　light=COMP=PFV　PART
　　　 'Waiting and waiting, and it was dawn.'

d 我啊晕嘀。
   ŋa   ỹ   ti.
   1:DAT   dizzy   PART
   'I am dizzy.'
e 玉林的阿大官当着嘀。
   ylĩ=tʁ   ata   kuã   tã=tʂʁ   ti.
   PN=GEN   father   official   assume=PROG   PART
   'Yulin's father is an official.'

Example (40a) can be used to emphasize that a dog lived a long time. The common sense suggests that a dog may not live for 20 years, but the speaker emphasizes that what he says is true and that he is quite sure about it. Examples (40b)–(40c) are accounts of past facts. If *ti* is not used, these sentences are still acceptable, unless the certainty tone that *ti* presents is less. Example (40d) can emphasize that the fact "I am dizzy" is certain, and therefore *ti* is used. Example (40e) describes a continuous state, and *ti* is also used to indicate a high degree of truth.

The previous examples are typical cases where *ti* appears. Since the function of *ti* is to express a high degree of certainty about what is being said or to emphasize that what is being said is real, it is most naturally used to describe what has happened. In examples (40a)(40c), *ti* coexists with the perfective marker =*lɔ*. In addition, *ti* may be used in other contexts, like these:

(41) a 扁食啊煮上了吃时香嘀。
        piãʂi=a   tʂu=xã=lɔ   tʂhi   ʂi   ɕiã   ti.
        dumpling=ACC   boil=COMP=PFV   eat   COND   fragrant   PART
        'Dumplings are delicious if you cook them.'
     b 今儿我啊做头多着很嘀，东西买去，还饭做掉嘀。
        tɕiɛ   ŋa   tsuʁthu   tuʁ=tʂʁ=xʁ̃   ti,   tũɕi   mɛ
        today   1:DAT   do   many=COMP=very   PART   thing   buy
        tɕhi,   xã   fã   tsi=tiɔ   ti.
        go   also   food   do=COMP   PART
        'I have a lot to do today, e.g., shopping and cooking.'

Example (41a) is a hypothetical conditional sentence in which the property expressed by *ʂi* 'fragrant' is caused by the action expressed by *tʂu* 'boil'. Example (41b) describes what is intended to be done and which has not happened yet. However, *ti* has a more certain sense of what is said: in (41a), when the condition expressed by the verb *tʂu* 'boil' is fulfilled, it is fairly certain that the dumplings are delicious; in (41b), the speaker is also quite certain about what he will do during the day.

Occasionally, *ti* can be used in interrogative sentences, for example:

(42) 什么响着嘀？
    ʂỹmʁ   ɕiã=tʂʁ   ti?
    what   rattle=PROG   PART
    'What is rattling?'

Example (42) is not a genuine question, but rather expresses a tone of dissatisfaction. The context of (42) could be that one hears a loud noise outside during one's nap and complains to oneself. For a genuine question, the sentence 什么响着个？ ʂỹmʁ ɕiã=tʂʁ kʁ? is preferred.

6.6.2 pa

pa 吧 is used in declarative and interrogative sentences, mainly to express a speculative mood, i.e., to speculate on what has happened or what will happen based on certain facts. For example:

(43) a 婆婆公公们啊一嗒坐的吧，我喂着没。
      phʁphʁ   kŭkŭ=ma   ita   tsuʁ   tʁ   pa,   ŋʁ
      mother-in-law father-in-law together live   PART PART 1
      ui=tʂʁ   mi.
      feed=PROG NEG
      'Perhaps living with my mother-in-law and father-in-law, I did not feed (the pigs).'
   b 胡小琴学里去了吧。
      xuɕiɔtɕhĩ   ɕyʁ=li   tɕhi=lɔ   pa.
      PN   school=LOC go=PFV   PART
      'Hu Xiaoqin may have gone to school.'
   c 早晨天晴着哩吧。
      tsɔʂʁ̃   thiã   tɕhĩ=tʂʁ   li   pa.
      tomorrow   weather sunny=PROG PART PART
      'It may be sunny tomorrow.'
   d 快四点了个，扎西来下的 mare 吧。
      khuɛ   si=tiã=lɔ   kʁ,   tʂaɕi   lɛ=xʁ=tʁ
      almost four=o'clock=PFV PART PN   come=COMP=NOMZ
      ma   ɉi   pa.
      NEG   COP   PART
      'It's almost four o'clock, and I am afraid that Zhaxi will not be able to come.'

e 扎西的娃娃心疼吧，扎西长得俊哩喤。
   tṣaɕi=tr uaua ɕĩthĩ̃   pa, tṣaɕi tṣã=tr=tɕỹ
   PN=GEN child good_looking PART PN   look=COMP=handsome
   li   xuã.
   PART   PART
   'Zhaxi's child should be good looking, (because) Zhaxi is good-looking.'
f 再饭啊一碗吃，没饱吧？
   tsɛ   fã=a   i   uã   tʂhi, mɨ   pɔ   pa?
   again food=ACC one bowl eat   NEG full PART
   'Have another bowl of food, not full, right?'

Example (43a) is a sentence pronounced by a woman who recalled her past life. Asked by me whether she used to feed pigs herself, she said that she used to live with her parents-in-law and did not feed pigs herself. The particle *pa* conveys an uncertain and speculative tone, indicating that what the speaker remembers (expressed by the first clause) is not that accurate. (43b) is also a supposition as to what happened. The speaker is unsure where Hu Xiaoqin has gone, so he uses *pa*. Example (43c) is a supposition about an event that has not yet occurred. The speaker may speculate that the weather will be fine the next day based on certain signs (e.g., the stars). Example (43d) is also a speculation about something that has not happened yet. Example (43e) illustrates the process of speculation through a current fact: Zhaxi is good looking and the supposition is that Zhaxi's child is good looking (the speaker has not seen Zhaxi's child), thus *pa* is used. In (43f), *pa* is used in a question and awaits an affirmative response from the speaker. This shows that there is a correlation between supposition and questioning and that the correlation lies in the uncertainty.

In addition to expressing supposition, *pa* can also be used in euphemistic expressions like the following:

(44) 肉香是香嘛，点儿贵了吧。
     ȵu   ɕiã   ʂi   ɕiã   ma,   tie   kuɨ=lɔ   pa.
     meat fragrant   COP fragrant   PART   little expensive=PFV   PART
     'Meat is delicious, but it might be a bit expensive.'

This function should also be related to the uncertainty that *pa* usually conveys.

6.6.3 li

li 哩 has three functions. First, *li* can be used in declarative sentences, simply to express the tone of a statement, exclamation, etc. For example:

(45) 电脑买时钱花着很哩。
 tiãnɔ   mɛ   ʂi   tɕhiã   xua=tʂɤ=xɻ̃   li.
 computer buy COND money   spend=COMP=very PART
 'It is a lot of money to spend if you buy a computer.'

(46) 箇我啊有时候好着很哩，有时候不好哩。
 kuɤ   ŋa   iuʂixɯ   xɔ=tʂɤ=xɻ̃   li,
 3   1:DAT   sometimes   good=COMP=VERY   PART
 iuʂixɯ   pu   xɔ   li.
 sometimes   NEG   good   PART
 'S/he sometimes treats me well, sometimes not.'

(47) 箇最公当哩。
 kuɤ   tsui=kũtã   li.
 3   most=fair   PART
 'S/he is the fairest.'

In (45), *li* carries an exclamatory tone. The particle can also be used directly after an adjective, as in *pu xɔ li* 'not good' (46) and *kũtã li* 'fair' (47).

The second function of *li* is to express that a given action is in progress. In this case the particle is attached to a verb. For example:

(48) 嘴啊张了什么做哩？
 tsui=a   tʂã=lɔ   ʂɻ̃mɤ   tsi   li?
 mouth=ACC   open=PFV   what   do   PART
 'What are you doing with your mouth open?'

(49) 扎西的脸红了着，一句话不说哩。
 tʂaɕi=tɤ   niã   xũ=lɔ=tʂɤ,   i=tɕy   xua   pu   ʂuɤ   li.
 PN=GEN   face   red=PFV=PROG   one=CL   word   NEG   say   PART
 'Zhaxi's face reddened and he did not say a word.'

(50) 饭吃着哩，电视看着，吃撒喤！
 fã   tʂhi=tʂɤ   li,   tiãsi   khã=tʂɤ,   tʂhi   sa   xuã!
 food   eat=PROG   PART   TV   watch=PROG   eat   PART   PART
 'You are watching TV when you eat. Eat quickly!'

Thirdly, *li* can be used as a future aspect marker (see Section 4.2.2). For example:

(51) a 我学里去哩。
     ŋɤ   ɕyɤ=li   tɕhi   li.
     1   school=LOC   go   PART
     'I am going to school.'

b 我学里去了。
   ŋɤ   ɕyɤ=li   tɕhi=lɔ.
   1   school=LOC   go=PFV
   'I went to school.'

The function of *li* as a future aspect marker is best demonstrated in the contrast between (51a) and (51b). The use of *li* in (51a) serves to indicate that "I will go to school", while the use of the perfective *lɔ* in (51b) serves to indicates that "I have already been to school".

The last two functions of *li* (i.e., indicating that an action is in progress and acting as a future marker) form a continuum and are clearly separated in their typical usage, showing that that distinction between the two functions is objective, although there are transitional situations between them. For example, *li* in the following example can be understood as a final particle without contentful meaning as a marker to convey "in progress" and as a future marker.

(52) 你什么吃的心有哩?
      ni   ʂɤ̃mɤ   tʂhi=tɤ   ɕĩ   iu   li?
      2   what   eat=REL   heart   have   PART
      'What do you want to eat?'

Example (52) asks what the hearer wants to eat, with the implication that the action of eating is yet to happen. Thus, *li* here can be interpreted as a future marker. At the same time, the predicate *tʂhi=tɤ ɕĩ iu* does not express a typical action, but rather a state, so *li* can also be interpreted to convey the meaning of "in progress". Also, it can be understood as a particle simply expressing a declarative tone.

6.6.4 xuã

The particle *xuã* 喤 appears only in sentence-final position and is used to strengthen the tone of a sentence. For example:

(53) 手啊放开撒，抓住了什么做哩，放开撒喤!
      ʂu=a   fã=khɛ   sa,   tʂua=tʂhu=lɔ   ʂɤ̃mɤ   tsi   li,
      hand=ACC   loose=COMP   PART   catch=COMP=PFV   what   do   PART
      fã=khɛ   sa   xuã!
      loose=COMP   PART   PART
      'Let go of your hands! What are you holding on? Let go!'

(54) 鼻子啊嫑吸着进去的喤，搛掉撒。
      pitsi=a   pɔ   ɕi=tʂɤ   tɕĩtɕhi   tɤ   xuã,
      snot=ACC   NEG:PROHIBIT   suck=COMP   in   PART   PART

       ɕĩ=tiɔ   sa.
       wipe=COMP   PART
       'Do not suck in the snot, wipe it off.'

(55) 你比林个讲的嗐。
       ni   *pilĩ=kɤ*   *tɕiã*   *tɤ*   *xuã.*
       2   story=CL   tell   PART   PART
       'You tell a story.'

(56) 你消停吃呀嗐！
       ni   *ɕiɔthĩ*   *tʂhi*   *ia*   *xuã!*
       2   slowly   eat   PART   PART
       'Eat slowly!'

(57) 个医生不是时就护士 re 呀嗐。
       kɤ *isɤ̃*   *pu* *ʂi* *ʂi*   *tɕiu* *xuʂi* *ɖi* *ia* *xuã.*
       this doctor NEG COP COND then nurse COP PART PART
       'This man is a nurse if he is not a doctor.'

(58) 三百六十天，净劳动着嘀嗐。
       sã   *pɨ*   *liuʂi*   *thiã,* *tɕĩ* *lɔtũ=tʂɤ*   *ti*   *xuã.*
       three hundred PART   day   all   labor=PROG PART PART
       'Three hundred and sixty days are spent in labor.'

From the previous examples, we can see that *xuã* cannot be used as a final particle alone but must appear after another particle. This shows that one of the characteristics of *xuã* is that it is always at the outermost component of a sentence. *xuã* contributes little to the truth-value semantics and is used by the speaker only to strengthen the tone. In (53)–(56), *xuã* is used after the particles *sa*, *tɤ* and *ia*, strengthening the tone of the imperative. This is a common use of *xuã*. In (57–58), *xuã* is used in declarative sentences to strengthen the tone and express subjective emotions of the speaker. For example, in (58) the speaker emphasizes that he works all year round, highlighting the long hours of labor, and *xuã* conveys a subtle feeling of dissatisfaction and disbelief.

6.6.5 kɤ

The particle *kɤ* 个 is used in declarative and interrogative sentences as a "neutral" final particle without conveying any special semantic or emotional meaning. For example:

(59) 水提提里满着个。
 ʂuitshitshi=li   mã=tʂɤ   kɤ.
 bucket=LOC   full=PROG   PART
 'The bucket is full.'

(60) 一滴儿两滴儿这么下着个。
 i=tiɛ   liã=tiɛ   tʂɤmɤ   ɕia=tʂɤ   kɤ.
 one=CL   two=CL   this_way   drop=PROG   PART
 'The rain fell one or two drops at a time.'

(61) 一扇门关着个，一扇门开着个。
 i=ʂã   mɤ̃   kuã=tʂɤ   kɤ,   i=ʂã   mɤ̃   khɛ=tʂɤ   kɤ.
 one=CL door close=PROG   PART one=CL door open=PROG   PART
 'One door is closed, and one door is open.'

(62) 罪犯下了个。
 tsui   fã=xɤ=lɔ   kɤ.
 crime   commit=COMP=PFV   PART
 'Committed a crime.'

(63) 扎西鸡娃宰下了个。
 tʂaɕi   tɕiua   tsɛ=xɤ=lɔ   kɤ.
 PN   chicken slaughter=COMP=PFV   PART
 'Zhaxi slaughtered the chicken.'

(64) 尕猫娃老鼠抓去了个。
 ka   mɔua   lɔtʂhu   tʂua   tɕhi=lɔ   kɤ.
 small   cat   rat   catch   go=PFV   PART
 'The kitten went to catch the mouse.'

(65) 俊着花般有个。
 tɕỹ=tʂɤ   xua=pã   iɔ   kɤ.
 good_looking=PROG   flower=POST   have   PART
 'Handsome like a flower.'

(66) 你啊什么吃的心有个？
 nia   ʂɤ̃mɤ   tʂhi=tɤ   ɕĩ   iɔ   kɤ?
 2:DAT   what   eat=REL   heart   have   PART
 'What do you want to eat?'

(67) 酒一盅盅儿有个。
  tɕiu i=tʂũtʂɤ iɔ kɤ.
  wine one=CL have PART
  'There is a glass of wine.'

The previous examples show three different combinations of *kɤ* with *tʂɤ*, *lɔ* and *iɔ*, which are the only particles with which *kɤ* can be used. After *tʂɤ* and *lɔ*, *kɤ* can also be omitted without changing the sense of the sentence. After *iɔ*, *kɤ* cannot be omitted. For example, *tɕỹ=tʂɤ xua=pã iɔ* is not acceptable. In this case, one can also replace *kɤ* with *li*, indicating that the use of *kɤ* is as analogous to the use of *li* in this case, which is just to express the declarative mood of the statement, without any special meaning.

6.6.6 ta

The particle *ta* 哒 is probably an amalgamated combination of the particles 的 *tɤ* and 啊 *a*. It is commonly used in imperative and declarative sentences, as seen in (68) and (69), respectively.

(68) a 给掉，我一个看哒。
    kɨ=tiɔ, ŋɤ i=kɤ khã ta.
    give=COMP 1 one=CL look PART
    'Give it to me, I will take a look.'
  b 你我啊钱给哒。
    ni ŋa tɕhiã kɨ ta.
    2 1:DAT money give PART
    'You give me money.'
  c 再一杯倒给哒。
    tsɛ i=pɨ tɔ=kɨ ta.
    again one=CL pour=VIM PART
    'Pour another glass of water.'

(69) a re 吗？这么说着哒。
    ʈɨ mɤ? tʂɤmɤ ʂuɤ=tʂɤ ta.
    COP Q this_way say=PROG PART
    'Is it right to say like this?'
  b 你机灵是机灵着很哩哒。
    ni tɕiliu ʂi tɕiliu=tʂɤ=xɤ̃ li ta.
    2 clever COP clever=COMP=very PART PART
    'You are very clever.'

In imperative and declarative sentences, the tone conveyed by *ta* can be interpreted as "determination": when used in imperative sentences, it is a "determination" of the content of the imperative, and when used in declarative sentences, it is a "determination" of what is stated.

6.6.7 ia

The particle *ia* 呀 is normally used in imperative sentences. For example:

(70) 再馍馍一个吃呀。
    tsɛ   mɤmɤ   i=kɤ   tʂhi   ia.
    again steamed_bread one=CL eat   PART
    'Have another steamed bread.'

(71) 你消停吃呀喧。
    ni   ɕiɔthĩ   tʂhi   ia   xuã.
    2   slowly   eat   PART   PART
    'You take your time to eat.'

ia in (70) is used alone, while in (71) it co-occurs with another particle, *xuã*. Although it is possible to use *ia* in imperative sentences, the more important function of this particle is to convey some kind of emphasis. For example:

(72) 阿吉故意打的不是呀，没防着就打上了。
    atɕi kui   ta=tɤ   pu   ʂi   ia,   mɨ   fã=tʂɤ
    3   purposively hit=NOMZ NEG COP PART NEG defend=PROG
    tɕiu   ta=xã=lɔ.
    then   hit=COMP=PFV
    'S/he did not mean to hit (it); s/he did not pay attention and hit (it).'

(73) 毛衣毛衣叫着嘀呀。
    mɔi   mɔi   tɕiɔ=tʂɤ   ti   ia.
    sweater sweater call=PROG   PART PART
    'A sweater is called a sweater.'

(74) 兀个，兀个呀，卫生院。
    ukɤ,   ukɤ,   ia,   uisĩyã.
    that   that   PART   health_center
    'That. That. The health center.'

(75) 个洋疯子个饭啊倒掉了。饭哈呀倒掉了。
kɤ   iã́fɤ̃tsi kɤ   fã=a   tɔ=tiɔ=lɔ.   fã=xa   ia
this lunatic this food=ACC dump=COMP=PFV   food=ACC PART
tɔ=tiɔ=lɔ.
dump=COMP=PFV
'This lunatic dumped the food. It was the food that has been dumped.'

In (72), *ia* is used to emphasize the clause in which it occurs, i.e., "S/he did not hit the man on purpose". In (73), *ia* is used with the particle *ti*. As mentioned in Section 6.6.1, *ti* has an emphatic function. The use of *ia* reinforces this function of *ti*. Example (74) shows *ukɤ* as it is often used in conversation to fill in the gaps when the speaker cannot think of an expression at the moment. In this example, the speaker wants to say *uisɤ̃yã*. 'health center' and may have it on his lips, but there is a tip-of-the-tongue effect and he just cannot remember how to say it at the moment. The speaker uses *ia* to emphasize "That is what I am going to say!" Example (75) was often pronounced in contexts where I, in the course of a survey, repeatedly asked the speaker because I did not understand what the speaker was saying. The speaker got impatient and used "X + *ia*" to express "I am saying X, why do not you understand?" In (75), the core function of *ia* is still emphatic, but in this context the whole sentence also has an intensified tone, which is specifically expressed by *ia*. Note that since *fã* is the focal component in the second repetition, the full form of accusative marker =*xa* (not =*a*) is used.

6.6.8 mɤ

mɤ is used as a question particle at the end of a yes-no question and as an interrogative disjunctive coordinator. For example:

(76) 你苹果吃了么？
ni   phĭkuɤ   tʂhi=lɔ   mɤ?
2   apple   eat=PFV   Q
'Did you eat apples?'

(77) 你去哩么小宋街上县城去哩？
ni   tɕhi li   mɤ   ɕiɔ   sũ   kɛ=xã   tɕhi li?
2   go   PART DISJ little Song   street=LOC   go   PART
'Are you or little Song going to the street?'

Minor word classes 101

The two uses of *mɤ* are discussed in Sections 7.6.1 and 6.8.2, respectively.

6.6.9 pɨ

The particle *pɨ* 呗 is mainly used to express a tone in which the speaker considers a fact to be obvious or taken for granted and can be sometimes used to express other tones depending on the context. For example:

(78) a 你靠酒喝上了呗？
      ni   khɔ   tɕiu   xuɤ=xã=lɔ   pɨ?
      2   again wine drink=COMP=PFV PART
      'You have started drinking again!'
   b 鱼鱼缸里有哩呗。
      y   ykã=li   iu   li   pɨ.
      fish fishbowl=LOC exist PART PART
      'The fish is in the fishbowl.'
   c 喝个几天你忙呗，天天忙呗，饭不吃来。
      tɤ   kɤ   tɕi   thiã   ni   mã   pɨ   thiãthiã
      DM   this several day   2   busy PART every_day
      mã   pɨ,   fã   pu   tʂhi   lɛ.
      busy PART meal NEG eat   come
      'You are busy every day during these days and do not come to dinner.'
   d 你说，嘴兰说呗。
      ni   ʂuɤ,   tsui=lã   ʂuɤ   pɨ.
      2   say   mouth=INS say   PART
      'You say, just say it with your mouth.'

In (78a), the speaker is sure of her statement based on the smell of alcohol or hearing about it, etc. By using *pɨ*, the speaker treats the matter as a known fact. In this specific context, the speaker can take on a discontented tone. In the context of (78b), I asked how to say in Zhoutun "The fish is in the fishbowl". In the speaker's opinion, it is obvious that it should be said this way, so *pɨ* is used. In (78c), the speaker thinks that the listener has been busy in the past few days and explains why the listener is not coming to dinner. In (78d), *pɨ* is employed in an imperative sentence where the speaker asks the hearer to speak and adds, "Just say it with your mouth!" It is natural to speak with the mouth, so *pɨ* is used to express the speaker's dissatisfaction and other tones.

6.6.10 sa

The particle *sa* 撒 has two main functions. First, it indicates that the information expressed by the constituent to which it is added is obvious. In other words, *sa* encodes background information. For example:

(79) 粮食兰换，西红柿啊换上时，西红柿好看撒，红着。个啊换上了吃时，浓呛着个。
liãʂi=lã xuã, ɕixũsi=a xuã=xã ʂi, ɕixũsi
grain=INS exchange tomato=ACC exchange=COMP when tomato
xɔkhã sa, xũ=tʂɤ. ka xuã=xã=lɔ tʂhi
good_looking PART red=PROG this:ACC exchange=COMP=PFV eat
ʂi, nũ tɕhiã=tʂɤ kɤ.
when strong_flavor choke=PROG PART
'(We) traded grain for tomatoes. Tomatoes look good. They are red. (But) it is too choking to eat tomatoes.'

(80) 二叔工打了来了撒，娃娃们哈炮仗给掉了着，郭咤的我没看了个。
ɤʂu kũ ta=lɔ lɛ=lɔ sa, uaua=mɤ=xa
second_uncle job work=PFV come=PFV PART child=PL=DAT
phɔtʂã kɨ=tiɔ=lɔ=tʂɤ, kuɤ=tha=tɤ ŋɤ mɨ
firecracker give=COMP=PFV=PROG there=ABL=REL 1 NEG
khã=lɔ kɤ.
watch=PFV PART
'Second uncle[8] came back from work and brought firecrackers to the children, and from there I did not watch.'

(81) 箇巴里撒，我撒，许佳撒，我们就杏儿偷去了。
kuɤ pa=li sa, ŋɤ sa, ɕytɕia sa, ŋɤ=mɤ
that time=LOC PART 1 PART PN PART 1=PL
tɕiɯ xɤ thɯ tɕhi=lɔ.
just apricot steal go=PFV
'In the old days, me and Xujia, we went to steal apricots.'

The basic idea of (79) is that the speaker used to exchange grains for tomatoes, and once she ate them after the exchange, she found that the tomatoes were very difficult to eat. The underlined part in (79) provides background information that can be considered a speaker's explanation of why she wanted to change tomatoes. Example (80) contains what a speaker said to me about a TV series called *Second Uncle*. The speaker claims that, after seeing the second uncle (the protagonist in the TV series) come back from his job, he never watched the rest of the series. The underlined part of the example can be interpreted as the background information of "The second uncle bought firecrackers for the children". Example (81) refers to a story told to me by a speaker of Zhoutun. The underlined part of the example specifies the time and background of the story.

The particle *sa* also has an interactive subjective function, i.e., it establishes a connection between the speaker and the hearer, and with it the speaker expresses the sense of the expression "Listen to me, that is the way it is!", seeking approval from the hearer. In (79), for example, the speaker thinks the listener should agree with the sentence "Tomatoes look good". This function of *sa* makes it possible to expect an affirmative answer when it occurs in an interrogative sentence, as in the following example.

(82) 你三个 X 要着撒？
 ni   sã̄=kʏ   ɛkhʏsi   iɔ=tʂʏ   sa?
 2   three=CL   X   need=PROG   PART
 'You need to wear clothes of three Xs?'

This example is from a conversation between two speakers in front of my computer while purchasing clothes online. Speaker A asked speaker B if she wanted to buy clothing of the size three Xs. It is not a neutral question. A presumes that B wanted to buy XXX size clothes, and this sentence is just to confirm this presumption, expecting B's affirmative response.

The second interactive function of *sa* can be observed in imperative sentences. In this context the particle primarily expresses the tone of a command. For example:

(83) 清水里一个冲给撒！
 tɕhĩfi=li   i=kʏ   tʂhũ=ki   sa.
 clean_water=LOC   one=CL   wash=VIM   PART
 'Wash it in clean water!'

(84) 床单铺上撒，被啊捂上！
 tʂhuãtã   phu=xã   sa   pi=a   u=xã!
 sheet   put=COMP   PART   quilt=ACC   cover=COMP
 'Put on the sheet and cover the quilt over the bed!'

(85) 嘴啊张撒！
 tsui=a   tʂã   sa!
 mouth=ACC   open   PART
 'Open your mouth!'

(86) 手啊放开撒!抓住了什么做哩?放开撒喤!
ṣɯ=a   fã=khɛ   sa!   tṣua=tṣhu=lɔ   ṣʅ̃mʏ tsi li,
hand=ACC loose=COMP PART grab=COMP=PFV what   do PART
fã=khɛ   sa   xuã!
loose=COMP PART PART
'Let go of the hand! Why did you grab it? Let it go!'

See more on imperative sentences in Section 7.5.

6.6.11 Summary

Section 6.6 presented ten common final particles of Zhoutun. The type(s) of sentence in which they occur and their semantics are now schematically indicated in Table 6.2.

As can be seen, the final particles in Zhoutun have two major features: first, they have a variety of functions. Second, they are commonly used. In the data I collected, although I did not elaborate precise statistics, the frequency of final particles is very high. The high frequency reflects the prominent status of the final particles in Zhoutun.

Table 6.2 Ten common final particles

Final particles	Type of sentence	Semantics and functions
ti	declarative	high degree of certainty
pa	declarative; interrogative	supposition
li	declarative; interrogative	certain intonation; in progress; future
xuã	imperative; declarative	strengthen the intonation
kʏ	declarative; interrogative	certain intonation
ta	imperative; declarative	certain intonation
ia	imperative; declarative	emphasis
mʏ	interrogative	question; disjunction
pi	declarative	"obvious"; background information; interactive subjectivity
sa	declarative; imperative	stronger intonation

6.7 Adpositions

Zhoutun has a hybrid prepositional-postpositional pattern. This probably reflects the composite identity of Zhoutun: it has both the VO linguistic characteristics of Chinese (prepositions) and the characteristics of OV languages (postpositions).

6.7.1 Prepositions

6.7.1.1 uã 往

uã indicates the direction of the action: "to, towards". In most cases, *uã* is followed by a locative component that specifies a "relative" position such as *ʂã* 'up' and *ɕia* 'down'. This preposition cannot precede a location noun.

(87) 拉锁往下拉。
    lasuɤ   *uã*   *ɕia*   *la.*
    zipper   towards down   pull
    'Pull down the zipper.'

(88) 我（*往）学里去哩。
    ŋɤ   (* *uã*)   *ɕyɤ=li*   *tɕhi*   *li.*
    1   toward   school=LOC go   PART
    'I am going to the school.'

uã usually occurs in the construction 往 Adj/V 里 V "*uã* Adj/V=*li* V", literally meaning "to do something toward a certain direction" and being conventionalized to express the meaning "to do something to a certain degree". For example:

(89) 往紧里拧。
    uã   *tɕĩ=li*   *nĩ.*
    toward   tight=LOC   twist
    'Tighten it up (lit. to manipulate it toward a tight direction).'

(90) 往死里吃。
    uã   *si=li*   *tʂhi.*
    toward   death=LOC eat
    'Eat too much. (lit. let [someone] eat toward a dead direction).'

106 *Minor word classes*

6.7.1.2 iũ *"溮"*

iũ means 'along'. For example:

(91) 溮河滩往上兀里上去时，雪山到嘀。
    iũ   *xuɹthã*   *uã*   *ʂã*   *uli*   *ʂãtɕhi*   *ʂi,*
    along   riverbank   toward   up   there   up   COND
    ɕyʐʂã   *tɔ*   *ti.*
    snowy_mountain   arrive   PART
    'Walking up along the riverbank, you can arrive at the snowy mountain.'

(92) 溮个路直直走时，斜马浪到嘀。
    iũ   *kɹ*   *lu*   *tʂitʂi*   *tsu*   *ʂi,*   *ɕimalã*   *tɔ*   *ti.*
    along   this   road   straightly   walk   COND   PN   arrive   PART
    'Go straight along this road and you will arrive at Xiemalang.'

iũ is used infrequently. In many cases, where the meaning of "along" is intended, *iũ* is not used. For example:

(93) 边边里走。
    piãpiã=li   *tsu.*
    roadside=LOC   walk
    'Walk along the roadside.'

6.7.1.3 pa 把

pa is a frequently used multifunctional preposition (a disposal marker) in Mandarin Chinese as well as in Northwest Chinese dialects (Ren 2006; Li and Chappell 2013). In Zhoutun, however, the use of *pa* is strictly restricted: it can only occur in the imperative construction 你把你 V "*ni pa ni* V". For example:

(94) 你把你坐。
    ni   *pa*   *ni*   *tsuɹ.*
    2   DISP   2   sit
    'Have a seat!'

(95) 你把你的事情做。
    ni   *pa*   *ni=tɹ*   *sitɕhĩ*   *tsuɹ.*
    2   DISP   2=GEN   thing   do
    'Do your things!'

(96) 你把你慢慢儿吃。
 ni   pa   ni   mãmɤ   tʂhi.
 2   DISP 2   slowly eat
 'Take your time to eat!'

(97) 你把你的活慢慢儿干。
 ni   pa   ni=tɤ   phɤ   mãmɤ   kã.
 2   DISP 2=GEN   work   slowly   do
 'Take your time to do your work!'

Example (94) is the most common expression for "*ni pa ni* V" and is often heard in everyday speech. The second person pronoun *ni* can be replaced by noun phrases and the verb can be modified by an adverb, as in (95), (97) and (96)–(97), respectively.

Also note that "*ni pa ni* V" is used only in on-the-spot contexts. The pronoun *ni* cannot be replaced by a noun. In very restricted situations, other personal pronouns can appear, for example:

(98) 你把你坐，我把我坐，箇把箇坐。
 ni   pa   ni   tsuɤ,   ŋɤ   pa   ŋɤ   tsuɤ,   kuɤ   pa   kuɤ   tsuɤ.
 2   DISP 2   sit   1   DISP 1   sit   3   DISP 3   sit
 'You sit; I sit; (make) him/her sit.'

It is unacceptable to use a noun instead of the "*ni*" of (98), e.g., *扎西把扎西坐，玉林把玉林坐 *tʂaɕi pa tʂaɕi tsuɤ, ylĩ pa ylĩ tsuɤ* PN DISP PN sit, PN DISP PN sit.

The conversational meaning of "*ni pa ni* V" is "You just V, do not worry about anything else". For example, the context of (94) is that I was having dinner at the speaker's house and a guest was coming to visit, so I also got up to show courtesy. The speaker accompanied the guest and said the sentence in (94) to me. With this sentence, he wanted to express: "You just sit, do not mind others!"

6.7.2 Postpositions

6.7.2.1 tɕhiã 前

tɕhiã is used after a proper noun or a personal pronoun to refer to the place where the person or people indicated by the proper noun or personal pronoun live. For example:

(99) 扎西前狗娃有个。
 tʂaɕi   tɕhiã   kuua   iɔ   kɤ.
 PN   POST   dog   exist   PART
 'Zhaxi's family has a dog (lit. There is a dog with Zhaxi's family).'

108 *Minor word classes*

(100) 阿舅前地有哩。
　　　 atɕiu　tɕhiã　tshi　iu　li.
　　　 uncle　POST　field　exist　PART
　　　 'Uncle's family has land (lit. There is land in uncle's family).'

(101) 我刚箇们前去了。
　　　 ŋɤ　tɕiã　kuɤ=mɤ　tɕhiã　tɕhi=lɔ.
　　　 1　just　3=PL　POST　go=PFV
　　　 'I just went to their house.'

6.7.2.2 pã 般

pã means 'like'. For example:

(102) 懒猪般，头不洗。
　　　 lã　tʂu　pã,　thu　pu　ɕi.
　　　 lazy　pig　POST　head　NEG　wash
　　　 'Like a lazy pig, (he) does not wash his head.'

(103) 你般这么高的草摞着哩。
　　　 ni　pã　tʂɤmɤ　kɔ=tɤ　tshɔ　luɤ=tʂɤ.
　　　 2　POST　this　tall=REL　grass　stack=PROG
　　　 'The grass of your height is stacking there.'

(104) 俊着花般有个。
　　　 tɕỹ=tʂɻ̃　xua　pã　iɔ　kɤ.
　　　 beautiful=COMP　flower　POST　have　PART
　　　 'Beautiful as a flower.'

(105) 阿吉我般这么胖哩么？
　　　 atɕi　ŋɤ　pã　tʂɤmɤ　phã　li　mɤ?
　　　 3　1　POST　this　fat　PART　Q
　　　 'Is s/he as fat as I am?'

6.8 Coordinators

Zhoutun has one conjunctive coordinator *tɛ* and two disjunctive coordinators, namely, the prepositional standard coordinator *puʂi*, and the postpositional, interrogative coordinator *mɤ*.

6.8.1 Conjunctive coordinator

The conjunctive coordinator of Zhoutun is *tɛ* 带. For example:

(106) 我带小宋兰两个街道里去了。
ŋɤ   tɛ   ɕiɔ   sũ   liã=kɤ   kɛtɔ=li   tɕhi=lɔ.
1   CONJ little Song two=CL   street=LOC   go=PFV
'Little Song and I went to the street.'

(107) 扎西带小宋两个婚结上了。
tʂaɕi tɛ   ɕiɔ   sũ   liã=kɤ   xũ   tɕiɛ=xã=lɔ.
PN   CONJ little Song two=CL   marriage   marry=COMP=PFV
'Zhaxi and Little Song got married.'

(108) 扎西带小宋的媒人。
tʂaɕi tɛ   ɕiɔ   sũ=tɤ   miɻĩ.
PN   CONJ little Song=GEN   matchmaker
'Matchmaker for Zhaxi and Little Song.'

(109) 常牧带东沟合并上了。
tʂhãmu   tɛ   tũkɯ   xuɤpĩ=xã=lɔ.
PN   CONJ PN   merge=COMP=PFV
'Changmu town and Donggou town were merged.'

(110) 个子我带你两个，我大哩。
kɤtsi   ŋɤ   tɛ   ni   liã=kɤ,   ŋɤ   ta   li.
height   1   CONJ   2   two=CL   1   tall PART
'Me and you, I am taller.'

The previous examples show that *tɛ* can link nouns and pronouns. Based on the following facts, *tɛ* is a conjunctive coordinator rather than a comitative preposition. First, the position of the coordinands can be switched. For example, *ŋɤ tɛ ɕiɔ sũ* is grammatically equivalent to *ɕiɔ sũ tɛ ŋɤ*. Second, adverbials can only occur outside the conjunctive construction as a whole. In (109), for example, temporal adverbial 昨儿 *tshuɤ* 'yesterday' could occur in front of the whole sentence, but it could not be placed between *tʂhãmu* and *tũkɯ*. If *tshuɤ* occurs after *tʂhãmu*, then *tɛ* should be deleted, as in *tʂhãmu tshuɤ tũkɯ=xa xuɤpĩ=xã=lɔ*. Finally, the coordinands linked by *tɛ* cannot be omitted. For example, (110) cannot be said as **kɤtsi ŋɤ tɛ ni liã=kɤ, ŋɤ ta li, tɛ tʂaɕi liã=kɤ, tʂaɕi ta li*.

110 *Minor word classes*

Another piece of evidence indicating that *tɛ* is a coordinator is that it can link verb phrases. Prepositions cannot do this.

(111) 我两个带碗洗，带音录。
      ŋɤ   liã=kɤ   tɛ   uã   ɕi,   tɛ   ĩ   lu.
      1   two=CL   CONJ   bowl   wash   CONJ   voice   record
      'We two are washing dishes and recording.'

6.8.2 Disjunctive coordinators

Zhoutun has two disjunctive coordinators: the prepositional, standard coordinator 不是 *puʂi* and the postpositional interrogative coordinator 么 *mɤ*.

The examples containing *puʂi* are listed here.

(112) a   不是个去，不是箇去。
         puʂi   kɤ   tɕhi,   puʂi   kuɤ   tɕhi.
         DISJ   this_place   go   DISJ   that_place   go
         'Go to this place or go there.'
      b   黑了走的巴，不是洋火点上，不是手电拿上。
         xi=lɔ   tsu=tɤ   pa,   puʂi   iãxuɤ   tiã=xã,
         dark=PFV   walk=NOMZ   when   DISJ   matchstick   light=COMP,
         puʂi   ʂutiã   na=xã.
         DISJ   flashlight   take=COMP
         'When walking in the evening, light a matchstick or take a flashlight.'
      c   扎西房子里有哩，不是街上有哩。
         tʂaɕi   fãtsi=li   iu   li,   puʂi   kɛ=xã   iu   li.
         PN   house=LOC   exist   PART   DISJ   street=LOC   exist   PART
         'Zhaxi is in the house or on the street (in the county).'

Three characteristics of the coordinator *puʂi* can be observed in these examples. First, *puʂi* can either occur in the beginning of each coordinand (112a, 112b) or be placed only in the last coordinand (112c). Second, the coordinands linked by *puʂi* are can only be clauses.[9] Noun phrases cannot be linked by *puʂi*. See (113):

(113) a   *安文栋，不是连珺街上有哩。
         *ãuɤtũ,   puʂi   liãtɕỹ   kɛ=xã   iu   li.
         PN   DISJ   PN   street=LOC   exist   PART
         'Anwendong or Lianjun is on the street (in the county).'

b   *箇，不是你饭吃来。
    *kuɤ,   puʂi   ni   fã   tʂhi   lɛ.
    3   DISJ   2   meal eat   come
    'S/he or you come to eat.'

Examples (113a) and (113b) are unacceptable unless the noun phrases they contain are replaced by clauses. For example:

(114) a   安文栋街上有哩，不是连珺街上有哩。
       ãuɤ̃tũ kɛ=xã   iu li, puʂi liãtɕỹ kɛ=xã   iu li.
       PN   street=LOC exist PART DISJ PN   street=LOC exist PART
       'Anwendong is on the street, or Lianjun is on the street.'
     b   箇饭吃来，不是你饭吃来。
       kuɤ fã   chi   lɛ,   puʂi ni fã   tʂhi   lɛ.
       3   meal eat   come DISJ 2   meal eat   come
       'S/he will come to eat, or you come to eat.'

The same is true for adjective phrase (AP) coordinands: the construction "AP_1, *puʂi*-AP_2" is not permitted unless APs are replaced by clauses. See (115):

(115) a   *箇苹果红，不是绿。
       *kuɤ phĩkuɤ xũ,   puʂi liu.
       that apple   red   DISJ   green
     b   箇苹果红红儿有个，不是绿绿儿有个。
       kuɤ phĩkuɤ xũxuɤ iɔ   kɤ, puʂi liulɛ   iɔ   kɤ.
       that apple   red_red have PART DISJ green_green have PART
       'That apple is red or green.'

Third, the coordinands linked by *puʂi* must be declarative clauses. They cannot be questions. Example (116) is thus ungrammatical:

(116) *安文栋来么,不是连珺来么？
     *ãuɤ̃tũ   lɛ   mɤ,   puʂi   liãtɕỹ   lɛ   mɤ?
     PN   come Q   DISJ   PN   come Q
     'Is Anwendong coming here, or is Lianjun coming here?'

Interrogative coordinands are exclusively linked by *mɤ* in Zhoutun, as shown next.

Since *puʂi* in the previous examples is always prepositional and definitely a Chinese form, one may wonder whether it is possible that *puʂi* is still a negative

112 *Minor word classes*

copula, like the formal Chinese counterpart. The answer to this question is no because in contemporary Zhoutun, a copula should occur in the final V-position, in accordance with the SOV order. This is clearly illustrated when the copula *ȵi*, borrowed from Amdo Tibetan, co-occurs with *puʂi* in the same clause.

(117) 扎西老师 re，不是学生 re。
      tʂaɕi   lɔsi   ȵi,   puʂi   ɕyʁsĩ   ȵi.
      PN   teacher COP   puʂi   student   COP
      'Zhaxi is a teacher or (he is) a student.'

Example (117) does not mean 'Zhaxi is a teacher but not a student', but rather 'Zhaxi is a teacher or a student'. The use of the (positive) copula *ȵi* indicates that *puʂi* cannot be a negative copula in this situation.[10]

Note that, in addition to being used as a disjunctive coordinator, *puʂi* can also appear in these two constructions: the *puʂi*-imperative construction and the *puʂi*-exceptive construction. See example (118) for the *puʂi*-imperative construction first.

(118)   The *puʂi*-imperative construction
      a   不是你个拿上。
         puʂi   ni   kɤ   na=xã.
         puʂi   2   this   take=COMP
         'Or you could take this.'
      b   不是我去哩喔。
         puʂi   ŋɤ   tɕhi li   uʁ.
         puʂi   1   go   PART PART
         'I am going to leave.'
      c   不是你山上甕去。
         puʂi   ni   ʂã=xã   pɔ   tɕhi.
         puʂi   2   mountain=LOC NEG:PROHIBIT go
         'You should not go to the mountain.'

In (118a), the addressee is a second-person singular, a canonical subject in an imperative sentence. Example (118b) is a first-person imperative construction.[11] Example (118c) shows that *puʂi* can also occur in a prohibitive sentence.

In the previous examples, *puʂi* somewhat softens the intensity of an imperative sentence. For example, compare (119), which does not contain *puʂi*, to (118a).

(119)   你个拿上。
        ni   kɤ   na=xã.
        2   this   take=COMP
        'You take this.'

Example (119), in most cases, expresses a command without soft tone. To reinforce the intensity of the command, a final particle with a sharp tone (such as *ia* or *sa*) can be added. When *puṣi* is used, as in (118a), the sentence is interpreted as an advice, and a strong final particle is unacceptable. See (120). The same is true for (118b) and (118c).

(120) a 不是你个拿上（*呀/撒）。
 puṣi ni kɤ na=xã (*ia/ sa).
 puṣi 2 this take=COMP PART
 'Or you could take this.'
 b 你个拿上呀/撒！
 ni kɤ na=xã ia/ sa!
 2 this take=COMP PART
 'You take this.'

Now let us discuss the *puṣi*-exceptive construction, shown in the following examples:

(121) The *puṣi*-exceptive construction
 a 三个不是没，拿上撒。
 sã=kɤ puṣi mɨ, na=xã sa.
 three=CL *puṣi* NEG take=COMP PART
 'There are only three; take them.'
 b 箇巴里饭馆一个不是没。
 kuɤ pa=li fãkuã i=kɤ puṣi mɨ.
 that time=LOC eatery one=CL *puṣi* NEG
 'At that time, there was only one eatery.'
 c 我三个不是没吃。
 ŋɤ sã=kɤ puṣi mɨ tʂhi.
 1 three=CL *puṣi* NEG eat
 'I ate only three.'
 d 姓周的我不是时没。
 ɕĩ tʂu=tɤ ŋɤ puṣi ʂi mɨ.
 surname Zhou=NOMZ 1 *puṣi* COND NEG
 'Only my surname is Zhou.'
 e 周屯里不是时没。
 tʂuthũ=li puṣi ʂi mɨ.
 Zhoutun=LOC *puṣi* COND NEG
 'Someone/something is only in Zhoutun.'
 f 大号不是时不成哩。
 ta xɔ puṣi ʂi pu tʂhɤ̃ li.
 large size *puṣi* COND NEG able PART
 'Only the large size is available.'

This construction is schematized as "NP *puṣi* (*ṣi*) NEG", in which *ṣi* is a conditional marker meaning "if" (< "when" < "time") and NEG stands for *mɨ* 'not have' in most cases and other negative morphemes occasionally. The conditional marker 时 *ṣi* is optional: when the noun phrase consists of a numeral phrase, *ṣi* is omitted; otherwise *ṣi* is used. The construction expresses the meaning of "only NP" by literally indicating that the alternatives or numbers of NPs are extremely small: if it is not NP, then nothing > the number of NP is small.

Now we turn to another disjunctive coordinator *mʌ*. It is an interrogative disjunctive coordinator, as we can see in the following examples.

(122)   苹果吃的心有个么,香蕉吃的心有个?
       phĩkuʌ tʂhi=tʌ ɕĩ iɔ kʌ mʌ ɕiãtɕiɔ tʂhi=tʌ
       apple eat=REL will have PART DISJ banana eat=REL
       ɕĩ iɔ kʌ.
       will have PART
       'Do you want to eat apples, or do you want to eat bananas?'

(123)   你去哩么扎西街上去哩?
       ni tɕhi li mʌ tʂaɕi kɛ=xã tɕhi li?
       2 go PART DISJ PN street=LOC go PART
       'Are you or Zhaxi going to the street (in the county)?'

In a few cases, *mʌ* breaks through the interrogative restriction and is allowed to appear in declarative contexts. See (124):

(124) a 雪下了,四天么五天下头有嘀。
            ɕyʌ ɕia=lɔ, si thiã mʌ u thiã ɕiathuu iu ti.
            snow fall=PFV four day DISJ five day drop exist PART
            'It has snowed for four or five days.'
      b 你我啊骂哩么打时,我啊气不上来哩。
            ni ŋa ma li mʌ ta ṣi, ŋa
            2 1:DAT scold PART DISJ hit COND 1:DAT
            tɕhi pu ṣãlɛ li.
            angry NEG come_up PART
            'Whether you scold me or hit me, I am not angry.'

For (124a), one may argue that the interrogative meaning is still traceable in that *si thiã mʌ u thiã* 'four days or five days' can be interpreted as a question that the addresser asks himself/herself. However, in (124b), the interrogative meaning is totally lost. Another noteworthy point is that *mʌ* links two noun phrases in (124a), although this use is rare in my data.

Minor word classes 115

mʏ is also a final question particle (see Section 6.6.8). Arguably, there is an evolving pathway "question particle > disjunctive coordinator", and this is particularly interesting because in literature only the opposite pathway has been signaled (Heine and Kuteva 2002; Kuteva et al. 2019). For the formation of the *puṣi* and *mʏ*, one can refer to Zhou (2021).

Notes

1 The function of *a-* in Zhoutun is twofold. First, it is a prefix used with nouns denoting relatives, e.g., *ata* 'father'. Second, it occurs in interrogative pronouns, e.g., *ali* 'where'. Please refer to Section 3.2.1.
2 There is no overt speech verb in *tha pu tɕhi*, but arguably, *tha* in this sentence refers to the IS "Zhaxi" rather than the NS "I" for two reasons. First, the speech verb *ṣuʏ* can be added in sentence-final position. Second, if *tha* refers to "I", semantically, this sentence would be awkward: line 3 is expected as an answer to line 2, thus, the words of line 3 are uttered by "Zhaxi" rather than a first-person singular subject.
3 *tha* is probably consciously identified as a Mandarin Chinese feature so that people try to avoid it in formal elicitation contexts.
4 If *tɕi* is replaced by a concrete number, say "three", with a rising tone, the sentences could only be a yes-no question ("Are there three persons who are coming tomorrow?" for [31a] and "Are there three benches and three tables?" for [31b]) but not a *wh-* question.
5 Note that *ṣi* is both in the list of coefficient numerals and digit numerals. For example, *ṣi* and *u-ṣi* are 'ten' and 'fifty', respectively. Here, fifty is broken into "five tens".
6 jin is a unit of weight in Chinese. 1 jin = 0.5 kg.
7 mu is a unit of area in Chinese. 1 mu ≈ 666.667 m^2.
8 A Chinese may have a number of uncles. "Second uncle" refers to the second oldest uncle. Here "Second uncle" is the title and the main character of the TV series *Second Uncle*.
9 Some languages distinguish clause- and verb phrase–coordinands by using different coordinators (Mithun 1988; Haspelmath 2004). Zhoutun does not make such a distinction.
10 If it is *ʑi* and *ṣi* that co-occur in a sentence, it is possible that they are both copulas. For example, Santa (a Mongolic language spoken in Gansu province) has two copulas: one is *we*, inherited, and the other is *shi*, borrowed from Mandarin Chinese. The two copulas can cooccur in a single sentence, leading to a double-marked clause (Grant 2012).
11 First-person imperatives are non-canonical (Aikhenvald 2010).

7 Clause structure

7.1 Word order

The basic word order in Zhoutun is SOV. Compared to other Sinitic varieties spoken in the Gan-Qing linguistic area, the SOV in Zhoutun is rigid rather than preferred (Zhou 2017). Zhoutun also has a number of word-order patterns that are in harmony with the OV order, while a few other patterns reflect the VO order (Dryer 1992).

(1) NP-adposition (OV) and adposition-NP (VO)
    a 阿舅前地有哩。
        atɕiu   *tɕhiã*   *tshi*   *iu*   *li.*
        uncle   POST   field   exist   PART
        'Uncle's family has land.'
    b 㳸个路直直走时，斜马浪到嘀。
        iũ   *kʅ*   *lu*   *tṣitṣi*   *tsu*   *ṣi,*   *ɕiɛmalã*   *tɔ*   *ti.*
        along this road straightly walk COND PN arrive PART
        'Go straight along this road and you will arrive at Xiemalang.'

(2) Predicate-copula (OV)
    扎西老师 re。
    tṣaɕi   *lɔsi*   *ɖi.*
    PN   teacher   COP
    'Zhaxi is a teacher.'

(3) Verb phrase-aspect (OV)
    我学里去了。
    ŋʅ   *ɕyʅ=li*   *tɕhi=lɔ.*
    1   school=LOC   go=PFV
    'I went to the school.'

(4) Verb phrase-negation (OV) and negation-verb phrase (VO)
    a   个房子大着没哩。
        kɤ   fãtsi   ta=tʂɤ=mi   li.
        this   house   big=PROG=NEG   PART
        'This house is not big.'
    b   早晨我不来哩。
        tsɔʂɤ̃   ŋɤ   pu   lɛ   li.
        tomorrow 1   NEG come PART
        'I will not come tomorrow.'

(5) Subject-question particle (OV)
    你苹果吃了么？
    ni   phĩkuɤ   tʂhi=lɔ   mɤ?
    2   apple   eat=PFV   Q
    'Did you eat apples?'

(6) Genitive-noun (OV)
    扎西的鼻子疼着个。
    tʂaɕi=tɤ   pitsi   thɤ̃=tʂɤ   kɤ.
    PN=GEN   nose   hurt=PROG PART
    'Zhaxi's nose hurts.'

(7) Relative clause-noun (OV)
    个子大着很的箇一个人来了。
    kɤtsi   ta=tʂɤ=xɤ̃=tɤ   kuɤ i=kɤ ɻɤ̃   lɛ=lɔ.
    stature tall=COMP=very=REL that one=CL person come=PFV
    'The person who is very tall came.'

(8) Comparative standard-adjective (OV)
    我你啊岁数大着嘀。
    ŋɤ   nia   suifu   ta=tʂɤ   ti.
    1   2:DAT age   old=PROG PART
    'I am much older than you.'

(9) Prepositional phrase-verb (OV)
    拉锁往下拉。
    lasuɤ   uã   ɕia   la.
    zipper   towards down   pull
    'Pull down the zipper.'

(10) Manner adverb-verb (OV)
你慢慢儿走。
ni mãmɤ tsɯ.
2   slowly walk
'You walk slowly.'

7.2 Ditransitive construction

A ditransitive construction contains a ditransitive verb V, an A(gent), a R(ecipient) and a T(heme) (Malchukov, Haspelmath, and Comrie 2010). In Zhoutun, the basic word order of ditransitive constructions is ARTV, with the dative marker =xa/=a added to the recipient. For example:

(11) 我箇啊书一本给了。
ŋɤ kua fu   i=pr̃ ki=lɔ.
1 3:DAT book one=CL give=PFV
'I gave him/her a book.'

(12) 扎西玉林哈饭一碗下给。
tʂaɕi ylĩ=xa fã   i uã ɕia=ki.
PN PN=DAT noodle one bowl cook=VIM
'Zhaxi cooked a bowl of noodles for Yulin.'

The theme usually does not need =xa/=a, but when it does not occur between the recipient and the verb, it can be marked by this enclitic. For example:

(13) 书哈扎西玉林哈一本给掉了。
fu=xa   tʂaɕi ylĩ=xa i=pr̃ ki=tiɔ=lɔ.
book=ACC PN PN=DAT one=CL give=COMP=PFV
'Zhaxi gave a book to Yulin.'

Another situation where the theme is marked by the enclitic =xa/=a is when the recipient is omitted. For example:

(14) 我地啊租给了。
ŋɤ tshi=a   tsy=ki=lɔ.
1 land=ACC rent=VIM=PFV
'I rented the land (to someone).'

Sometimes only the theme receives =xa/=a while the recipient is unmarked. For example:

(15) 我箇一个人头啊理给掉了。
 ŋɤ   kuɤ i=kɤ   ɖĩ   thuu=a   li=ki=tiɔ=lɔ.
 1   that one=CL person   hair=ACC cut=VIM=COMP=PFV
 'I gave that man a haircut.'

The predicates occurring in ditransitive constructions can be classified into three types: (i) the verb *ki* 给 'give' (as in [11]); (ii) V 给 V=*ki* (as in [12]); (iii) other verbs such as *tɕhiɔ* 乔 'treat' (16) and *na* 拿 'take' (17).

(16) 玉林全息我们啊火锅乔了。
 ylĩ   tɕhyãɕi   ŋɤ=ma   xuɤkuɤ   tɕhiɔ=lɔ.
 PN   last_night   1=PL:DAT   hot_pot   treat=PFV
 'Yulin treated us to hot pot last night.'

(17) 你我啊外头的箇碗拿上进来，我洗上。
 ni ŋa   uɛthu=tɤ   kuɤ   uã   na=xã   tɕĩlɛ, ŋɤ ɕi=xã.
 2   1:DAT   outside=GEN   that bowl take=COMP   come   1   wash=COMP
 'You bring me the outside bowls; I will wash them.'

Note the verb in the sequence V=*ki* cannot be *ki* itself.

(18) *你我啊书一本给给。
 *ni ŋa   fu   i=pɽ̃   ki=ki.
  2   1:DAT   book   one=CL   give=VIM
 'You give me a book.'

7.3 Copula clause

In Zhoutun the copula clause is "copula subject+complement+copula" (on a par with SOV). There are two copulas. One is *ɖi* (negated by *ma*: *ma ɖi*), borrowed from Amdo Tibetan, and the other is 是 *ʂi* (negated by *pu*: 不是 *pu ʂi*), inherited. Of the two, it can be claimed that *ɖi* is the unmarked copula, and *ʂi* is marked. This can be illustrated in the following aspects.

The first aspect is formal markedness. *ɖi* is used independently as a copula, while *ʂi* needs to be followed by a final particle. See (19) and (20).

(19) 扎西老师 re，医生 ma re。
 tʂaɕi   lɔsi   ɖi,   isɽ̃   ma   ɖi.
 PN   teacher   COP   doctor   NEG   COP
 'Zhaxi is a teacher, not a doctor.'

(20) a 猫娃动物是嘀。
   mɔua   tũu   ʂi   ti.
   cat   animal   COP   PART
   'A cat is a kind of animal.'
  b 个尽皆我们的不是呀。
   kɤ   tɕĩtɕɛ   ŋɤ=mɤ=tɤ   pu   ʂi
   this   all   1=PL=GEN   NEG   COP
   'None of these are ours.'

As shown in these two examples, *ɖi* can be used alone, whereas *ʂi* must be followed by a final particle.

The second aspect is pragmatic neutrality and textual frequency. *(ma) ɖi* is pragmatically neutral and has a high textual frequency. That is, in pragmatic neutral contexts, *(ma) ɖi* is preferred over *(pu) ʂi*. When native speakers are asked, for example, what is the most natural way to express 'I am a student', they say *ŋɤ ɕyɤsɻ̃ ɖi* (1 student COP). In contrast, *(pu) ʂi*, followed by a final particle that conveys various types of intonation (see Section 6.6 for detail), is not pragmatically neutral and not surprisingly has lower textual frequency.

The third aspect is syntactic distribution. *(ma) ɖi* has a wider syntactic distribution than *(pu) ʂi*, which is subject to certain restrictions. The first context in which the two copulas differ from each other is that in which the complement of the copular clause is a locative constituent. *ɖi* can be used in this context, while *ʂi* cannot.

(21) a 扎西家里 re。
   tʂaɕi   tɕia=li   ɖi.
   PN   home=LOC   COP
   'Zhaxi is at home.'
  b 包包儿桌上 re。
   pɔpɤ   tʂuɤ=xã   ɖi.
   bag   desk=LOC   COP
   'The bag is on the desk.'

In this context, *ɖi* is a locational copula, but *ʂi* is not allowed in such a case.

The asymmetry between *ɖi* and *ma ɖi* is noticeable. While *ɖi* can occur with a locative complement, *ma ɖi* cannot. The negative existential-possessive verb *mi* is employed in this context (as in (22)) and the existential-possessive verb *iu* is more common in the context shown in (21)—see (23).

(22) 扎西学里没。
    tʂaɕi   ɕyʀ=li   mɨ.
    PN   school=LOC   NEG
    'Zhaxi is not at school.'

(23) 阿吉庙上有。
    atɕi   miɔ=xã   iɯ.
    3   temple=LOC   exist
    'S/he is in the temple.'

Another context highlighting the different syntactic distribution of *(ma) ɬɨ* and *(pu) ʂi* is that in which a clause or a sentence is negated. Again, *(ma) ɬɨ* can occur in this context, whereas *(pu) ʂi* cannot. The following example illustrates this:

(24) a 扎西学里去了，re 么 ma re？
       tʂaɕi   ɕyʀ=li   tɕhi=lɔ,   ɬɨ   mʀ   ma   ɬɨ?
       PN   school=LOC go=PFV   COP   Q   NEG   COP
       'Zhaxi went to school, didn't he (lit. [it] is [the truth] or [it] is not)?'
    b re/ ma re.
       ɬɨ /   ma   ɬɨ.
       COP/   NEG   COP
       'Yes (lit. it is the truth)./No (lit. it is not the truth).'

In (24a), *ɬɨ mʀ ma ɬɨ* is a tag question about the truth value of the preceding clause. (24b) is the answer to (24a), with *ɬɨ* and *ma ɬɨ* occurring (alternatively) as a pro-sentence (Schachter and Shopen 2007, 31). Example (24b) can also be used as a response to a statement, such as to the first declarative clause of (24a). Both (24a) and (24b) do not allow the use of *(pu) ʂi*.

The third difference between *(ma) ɬɨ* and *(pu) ʂi* is that *ɬɨ* is omissible in certain situations, while *ʂi* cannot be omitted. See the following examples:

(25) 茶药兰一个话（re）。
    tʂha   yʀ=lã   i=kʀ   xua   (ɬɨ).
    tea   herb=COM   one=CL   word   (COP)
    'Tea and herb are one word.'

(26) 连珺丫头*（是）呀。
    liãtɕy̰   iathu   *(ʂi)   ia.
    PN   girl   COP   PART
    'Lianjun is a girl.'

In (25), *ȵi* is omissible, whereas *ʂi* is obligatory in (26). This distinction shows that *ȵi* is the default copula in Zhoutun, like *shi* in Mandarin, which is also omissible, as in *Zhangsan (shi) zhongguo ren* PN (COP) China people 'Zhangsan is Chinese'.

7.4 Comparative clause

7.4.1 Comparative construction

The comparative construction usually contains four constituents: the comparative subject (ComSub), the comparative standard (ComSt), the comparative marker (ComM) and the comparative result (ComR; usually an adjective). The ComR may indicate a concrete or abstract notion. The former is mostly expressed by a numeral or an adjective, while the latter notion is often expressed by a degree adverb. See two examples from Mandarin Chinese,

(27) a 张三比李四高一米。
    Zhangsan   *bi*   *Lisi*   *gao*   *yi*   *mi.*
    PN   CM   PN   tall   one   meter
    'Zhangsan is one meter taller than Lisi.'
  b 张三比李四高得多。
    Zhangsan   *bi*   *Lisi*   *gao*   *de*   *duo.*
    PN   CM   PN   tall   COMP   much
    'Zhangsan is much taller than Lisi.'

In (27), Zhangsan is the ComSub, Lisi is the ComSt, and *bi* is the ComM. In (27a), *gao yi mi* is a concrete ComR. In (27b), *gao de duo* is an abstract ComR.

7.4.1.1 The form of comparative constructions

There are two comparative constructions in Zhoutun and three comparative strategies used for expressing comparative meaning. Let us start from the two comparative constructions.
    I. ComSub + ComSt + ComM + ComR.
    The ComM is here 哈/啊 =*xa*/=*a*. For example:

(28) 个箇啊大着个。
    kɤ   *kua*   *ta=tʂɤ*   *kɤ.*
    this   that:DAT   big=PROG   PART
    'This is bigger than that.'

(29) 安文栋连珺哈三岁大着哩。
　　　ãuȓtũ　　liãtɕŷ=xa　　sã　　　suɨ　　ta=tʂȓ　　　li.
　　　PN　　　　PN=DAT　　three　year　old=PROG　　PART
　　　'Anwendong is three years older than Lianjun.'

(30) 我你啊岁数大着多。
　　　ŋȓ　　　nia　　　　ʂuɨfu　　ta=tʂȓ　　　　tuȓ.
　　　1　　　2:DAT　　age　　　old=COMP　　much
　　　'I am much older than you.'

Note that while a numeral expressing the concrete ComR occurs before the ComR adjective, a degree adverb expressing an abstract degree is placed after it. Thus, type I can be further divided into:

Ia. ComSub + ComSt + ComM + concrete number + ComR adjective
Ib. ComSub + ComSt + ComM + ComR adjective + abstract degree

Now we turn to type II, a less frequently used type than I.
　　II.　　ComSub + ComM + ComSt + ComR
　　The ComM here is 比 *pi*. For example:

(31) 个房子比郭房子大着个。
　　　kȓ　　　fãtsi　　pi　　　kuȓ　　fãtsi　　ta=tʂȓ　　　kȓ.
　　　this　　house　　CM　　that　　house　　big=PROG　　PART
　　　'This house is bigger than that.'

(32) 我比你大一岁。
　　　ŋȓ　　　pi　　　ni　　　ta　　　i　　　suɨ.
　　　1　　　CM　　　2　　　old　　one　　year
　　　'I am one year older than you.'

(33) 我比你大着多。
　　　ŋȓ　　　pi　　　ni　　　ta=tʂȓ　　　　tuȓ.
　　　1　　　CM　　　2　　　old=COMP　　much
　　　'I am much older than you.'

Based on (31)–(33), we can divide two subtypes of II:

IIa. ComSub + ComM + ComSt + ComR adjective + concrete number
IIb. ComSub + ComM + ComSt + ComR adjective + abstract degree

Now we turn to the three comparative strategies.

IIIa. "X *tɛ* Y (*liã=kʏ*), X/ Y ComR adjective". For example:

(34) 羊肉带大肉，羊肉香着个。
iãɻɯ   tɛ   taɻɯ,   iãɻɯ   ɕiã=tʂʏ   kʏ.
mutton   CONJ   pork   mutton   fragrant=PROG   PART
'Mutton is more delicious than pork (lit. between mutton and pork, mutton is delicious).'

(35) 我带扎西两个，扎西俊哩喔。
ŋʏ   tɛ   tʂaɕi   liã=kʏ,   tʂaɕi   tɕỹ   li   uʏ.
1   CONJ   PN   two=CL   PN   good_looking   PART   PART
'Zhaxi is more handsome than me (lit. between Zhaxi and I, Zhaxi is handsome).'

IIIb: "X *tɛ* Y V *ʂi*, X/Y V=*tʂʏ* Adj". For example:

(36) 我馍馍带面片儿吃时，馍馍吃着多。
ŋʏ   mʏmʏ   tɛ   miãphiɛ   tʂhi   ʂi,   mʏmʏ
1   steamed_bread   CONJ   noodle   eat   COND   steamed_bread
tʂhi=tʂʏ   tuʏ.
eat=COMP   more
'I eat more steamed breads than noodles (lit. when talking about eating steamed bread and noodles, I eat more steamed bread).'

IIIc: "X *khã=lɔ*, Y Adj". For example:

(37) 你们的房子看上了，我们的房子大。
ni=mʏ=tʏ   fãtsi   khã=xã=lɔ,   ŋʏ=mʏ=tʏ   fãtsi   ta.
2=PL=GEN   house   look=COMP=PFV   1=PL=GEN   house   big
'Our house is bigger than yours (lit. looking at your house, our house is bigger).'

(38) 安文栋的分数看了嘀，连珺的分数高哩。
ãuʏ̃tũ=tʏ   fʏ̃fu   khã=lɔ   ti,   liãtɕỹ=tʏ   fʏ̃fu   kɔ   li.
PN=GEN   score   look=PFV   PART   PN=GEN   score   high   PART
'Lianjun's score is higher than Anwendong's (lit. looking at Anwendong's score, Lianjun's is higher).'

In this latter strategy, X corresponds to the ComSt and Y to the ComSub. The comparative constructions I and II can be combined with the strategy III. For example:

(39) 我带扎西两个，扎西我啊大着个。
ŋɤ   tɛ   tʂaɕi   liã=kɤ   tʂaɕi   ŋa   ta=tʂɤ   kɤ.
1   CONJ   PN   two=CL   PN   1:DAT   old=PROG   PART
'Between Zhaxi and I, Zhaxi is older than me.'

(40) 我语文哈看了着，比数学好。
ŋɤ   yuɤ̃=xa   khã=lɔ=tʂɤ   pi   fuɕyɤ   xɔ.
1   Chinese=DAT   look=PFV=PROG   CM   math   better
'Looking at my Chinese, it is better than my math.'

7.4.1.2 *The topic property of comparative constructions*

Liu (2012b) points out that Chinese comparatives include not only a ComSub but also an attribute subject (AttSub) referring to some kind of attribute of the ComSub. The two types of subject often overlap but can also be separated. For example:

(41) 我钱比他多。
wo   qian   bi   ta   duo.
1   money   CM   3   more
'I have more money than him/her.'

In (41), the ComSub is *wo*, the ComSt is *ta*, while *qian* is the AttSub. The ComR *duo* is associated with the AttSub rather than the ComSub: it is *qian duo* 'more money' rather than *wo duo* 'more me'. Moreover, the ComSub and the ComSt do not need to be coreferential. In (41), the AttSub is *qian* 'money', whereas the ComSt is *ta* 'he/she'. Thus, (41) literally means "My money is more than him/her", which is unacceptable in English.

On the other hand, Chinese comparative constructions have the syntactic limitation that the subject (both ComSub and AttSub) and the ComSt should occur before the predicate. For example:

(42) a   *我比书更爱看电影。
         *wo   bi   shu   geng   ai   kan   dianying.
          1   CM   book   more   love   look   movie
     b   我书比电影更爱看。
         wo   shu   bi   dianying   geng   ai   kan.
          1   book   CM   movie   more   love   look
         'I love reading books more than watching movies.'

126 *Clause structure*

Example (42a), for example, is ungrammatical because the ComSt *dianying* occurs after the predicate verb.

In Zhoutun, the comparatives perform similarly: (i) they include a ComSub and an AttSub, as in (43); (ii) the AttSub and the ComSt do not need to be coreferential, as in (44); (iii) the subject and the ComSt can only occur before the predicate verb (as in both [43] and [44]). For example:

(43) 我你啊岁数大着嘀。
ŋɤ   nia   suifu   ta=tʂɤ   ti.
1   2:DAT   age   old=PROG   PART
'I am much older than you.' (ComSub= ŋɤ; AttSub= *suifu*)

(44) 你的鞋我啊一号大着哩。
ni=tɤ   xɛ   ŋa   i   xɔ   ta=tʂɤ   li.
2=GEN   shoe   1:DAT   one   size   big=PROG   PART
'Your shoes are one size bigger than mine.'

7.4.2 Comparative construction of equality

In Zhoutun, a comparative construction of equality can be productively formed by adding the word 一样 *iiã* 'the same' before the ComR. For example:

(45) 个树箇树哈一样大。
kɤ   fu   kuɤ   fu=xa   iiã   ta.
this   tree   that   tree=DAT   the_same   tall
'This tree is as tall as that one.'

7.4.3 Superlative construction

To form a superlative construction, the word *tsui* 最 'most' is used before the adjective. For example:

(46) 个花开时也最早哩说。
kɤ   xua   khɛ   ɕi   iɛ   tsui   tsɔ   li   ʂuɤ.
this   flower   bloom   time   also   most   early   PART   say
'It is said that this kind of flower is the earliest to bloom.'

7.5 Imperative clause

7.5.1 The form of imperative clauses

There is no dedicated morpheme used exclusively to form imperative clauses in Zhoutun, but a number of strategies are described in the following subsections.

7.5.1.1 "Zero marking"

With "zero marking", I refer to an imperative clause formed without any specific marker. For example:

(47) 米汤喝!
mithã   xuɤ!
rice_soup   drink
'Drink the rice soup!'

(48) 鞋啊脱下!
xɛ=a   thuɤ=xɤ
shoe=ACC   take_off=COMP
'Take off the shoes!'

(49) 你手啊洗去!
ni   ʂu=a   ɕi   tɕhi!
2   hands=ACC   wash   go
'Go wash your hands!'

7.5.1.2 V=kɨ

In a number of imperative clauses, the valency-increasing marker =kɨ (see Section 4.6) can be added to the verb. For example:

(50) 你我啊一碗舀给!
ni   ŋa   i   uã   iɔ=kɨ!
2   1:DAT   one   bowl   scoop=VIM
'Scoop a bowl (of water) for me!'

(51) 你名字啊签给!
ni   mĩtsi=a   tɕhiã=kɨ!
2   name=ACC   sign=VIM
'You sign your name!'

(52) 你头啊一个梳给!
ni   thu=a   i=kɤ   ʂu=kɨ!
2   head=ACC   one=CL   comb=VIM
'Comb your hair!'

As discussed in Section 4.6, V=kɨ is a valency-increasing device, not a specific way to impart order.

7.5.1.3 V tsɯ

The occurrence of *tsɯ* 走 'walk; go' after a verb is restricted to cohortative contexts, and there are, in addition, many restrictions on the use of the construction "V *tsɯ*". For example:

(53) 我两个看走!
    ŋɤ   liã=kɤ   khã   tsɯ.
    1   two=CL   look   go
    'Let's go have a look!'

(54) 象棋下走!
    ɕiãtɕhi   ɕia   tsɯ!
    chess   play   go
    '(Let's) go play chess!'

(55) 我两个饭吃走。
    ŋɤ   liã=kɤ   fã   tʂhi   tsɯ.
    1   two=CL   food   eat   go
    'Let's go for dinner!'

Examples (53)–(55) illustrate the restrictions that the use of *tsɯ* implies. First, the subject must be first-person plural. If the subject is second person, the construction "V *tɕhi* 'go'" must be used. If the subject is first person but singular, the construction "V *tsɯ*" is unacceptable, too. Second, the construction "V *tsɯ*" must involve spatial displacement. An action that does not have spatial displacement therefore cannot use this construction. For example, if two people were already seated at the dinner table and the speaker wished to express "Let's eat now!", the construction "V *tsɯ*" could not be used because there is no spatial displacement in this situation. Third, the construction "V *tsɯ*" does not have a negative form. Therefore, *我两个饭嫑吃走 *ŋɤ liã=kɤ fã pɔ tʂhi tsɯ* (1 two=CL food NEG.PROHIBIT eat walk) 'Let's do not go for dinner' is ungrammatical.

7.5.1.4 Final particles

Some final particles in Zhoutun (e.g., *sa*, *ta*, *ia*, *uɤ* and *xuã*) are often found in imperative clauses.

(56) 饭一满吃完撒!
    fã   imã   tʂhi=uã   sa!
    food   all   eat=finish   PART
    'Finish your meals!'

(57) 给掉!我一个看哒。
　　　ki̠=tiɔ!　　　ŋɤ　　i=kɤ　　　khã　　ta.
　　　give=COMP　1　　one=CL　　look　　PART
　　　'Give it to me! I will take a look.'

(58) 吃呀!
　　　tʂhi　　ia!
　　　eat　　PART
　　　'Eat!'

(59) 好好儿吃喔!
　　　xɔxɤ　　tʂhi　　uɤ!
　　　well　　eat　　PART
　　　'Eat well!'

(60) 你消停吃呀喤!
　　　ni　　ɕiɔthĩ　　tʂhi　　ia　　xuã!
　　　2　　slowly　　eat　　PART　　PART
　　　'Take your time to eat!'

7.5.1.5 ni pa ni V

你把你 V "*ni pa ni* V" is another construction that is used in imperative contexts. For example:

(61) 你把你坐!
　　　ni　　pa　　ni　　tsuɤ.
　　　2　　DISP　　2　　sit
　　　'Have a seat!'

(62) 你把你的事情做。
　　　ni　　pa　　ni=tɤ　　sitɕhĩ　　tsuɤ!
　　　2　　DISP　　2=GEN　　thing　　do
　　　'You do your things!'

See Section 6.7.1 for more discussion on this construction.

7.5.1.6 puṣi

As discussed in Section 6.8.2, the disjunctive coordinator 不是 *puṣi* can be placed at the beginning of an imperative sentence as an intonation-softening marker. Some examples follow.

130 *Clause structure*

(63) 不是你个提上.
    puʂi   ni   kɤ   tshi=xã.
    DISJ   2   this   carry=COMP
    'Or you could carry this!'

(64) 不是我去哩喔.
    puʂi   ŋɤ   tɕhi   li   uɤ.
    DISJ   1   go   PART   PART
    'Or let me go.'

7.5.1.7 *Rhetorical question*

In Zhoutun, the rhetorical question 不 V 么? *pu* V *mɤ?* can be used with a harsh tone for imparting an order. For example:

(65) 你不去么?
    ni   pu   tɕhi   mɤ?
    2   NEG   go   Q
    'You go!' (lit. Are you not going?)

(66) 连珺，你饭不吃吗?
    liãtɕỹ,   ni   fã   pu   tʂhi   mɤ?
    PN   2   meal   NEG   eat   Q
    'Lianjun, eat the meal!' (lit. Lianjun, don't you eat?)

7.5.2 *The negation of imperative clauses*

For the negative form of an imperative clause, the prohibitive marker 嫑 *pɔ* is used. For example:

(67) 你嫑去。
    ni   pɔ   tɕhi.
    2   NEG:PROHIBIT   go
    'Do not go.'

(68) 电视嫑看呀!
    tiãsi   pɔ   khã   ia!
    TV   NEG:PROHIBIT   watch   PART
    'Do not watch TV!'

Clause structure 131

7.6 Interrogative clause

7.6.1 Yes-no questions

In Zhoutun there are two ways for expressing a yes-no question: (i) by using the final question marker 么 *mɤ*, as in (69a), or (ii) by pronouncing a declarative sentence with a rising final intonation, as in (69b).

(69) a 扎西来了么?
     tʂaɕi   *lɛ*   *lɔ*   *mɤ?*
     PN   come   PFV   Q
   b 扎西来了?
     tʂaɕi   *lɛ*   *lɔ?*
     PN   come   PFV
     'Did Zhaxi come?'

7.6.2 Wh- *questions*

Wh- words are discussed in Section 6.3. In a *wh-* question, the *wh-* word occurs in the position of the noun/pronoun in the corresponding declarative sentence. For example:

(70)   阿个来了?
       akɤ   *lɛ=lɔ?*
       who   come=PFV
       'Who came?' (the *wh-* word is the subject)

(71)   扎西阿个啊钱给了?
       tʂaɕi   *aka*   *tɕhiɛ*   *ki=lɔ?*
       PN   who:DAT money   give=PFV
       'Who did Zhaxi give money to?' (the *wh-* word is the recipient)

(72)   扎西连珺啊什么给了?
       tʂaɕi   *liãtỹ=a*   *ʂɤmɤ*   *ki=lɔ?*
       PN   PN=DAT   what   give=PFV
       'What did Zhaxi give to Lianjun?' (the *wh-* word is the theme [object])

(73)   个阿个的书?
       kɤ   *akɤ=tɤ*   *fu?*
       this   who=GEN   book
       'Whose book is this?' (the *wh-* word is the genitive modifier)

132 *Clause structure*

Wh- words strictly occur before the verb. The following examples are thus unacceptable:

(74) *你吃，什么？
     *ni   tʂhi,   ʂɤmɤ?
     2   eat   what
     'What did you eat?'

(75) *苹果吃，阿个？
     *phĩkuɤ   tʂhi,   akɤ?
     apple   eat   who
     'Who ate the apple?'

7.6.3 Alternative question

An alternative question is one in which the speaker proposes two or more alternatives to the listener and the listener chooses one of them as the answer. An alternative question construction in Zhoutun is a construction of the type "X *mɤ* Y?" in which X is an interrogative clause, *mɤ* is the disjunctive coordinator, and Y may be a clause other than X or the negative form of X ("NEG (X)"). For example:

(76) I   X *mɤ* Y?
         你去哩么小宋街上去哩？
         ni   tɕhi   li   mɤ   ɕiɔ   sũ   kɛ=xã   tɕhi   li?
         2   go   PART   DISJ little   Song   street=LOC   go   PART
         'Will you go to the street or will Little Song go to the street?'
     II X *mɤ* neg (X)?
     a   早晨你街上去哩么不去？
         tsɔʂɤ̃   ni   kɛ=xã   tɕhi   li   mɤ   pu   tɕhi?
         tomorrow   2   street=LOC   go   PART   DISJ   NEG   go
         'Are you going to the street tomorrow?'
     b   你黑饭吃了吗没？
         ni   xifã   tʂhi=lɔ   mɤ   mi?
         2   dinner   eat=PFV   DISJ   NEG
         'Did you have dinner?'

7.6.4 Tag question

There are three main forms of a tag question in Zhoutun.

First, "declarative clause, *ɟi mɤ (ma ɟi)*?" For example:

(77) 这么说时成嘀，re 么？
tsɤmɤ	ʂuɤ	ʂi	tʂhɤ̃	ti,	ɟi	mɤ?
this_way	say	COND	able	PART	COP	Q

'It is okay to say this, right?'

(78) 扎西街上去了说，re 么 ma re?
tsaɕi	kɛ=xã	tɕhi=lɔ	ʂuɤ,	ɟi	mɤ	ma	ɟi?
PN	street=LOC	go=PFV	say	COP	DISJ	NEG	COP

'It was said that Zhaxi went to the street, right?'

The second way is "declarative clause, *la*?", which expects a positive answer. For example:

(79) 五六次也完的 ma re，啦？
u	liu=tshi	iɛ	uã=tɤ	ma	ɟi,	la?
five	six=CL	also	finish=REL	NEG	COP	TAG

'It cannot be used up five or six times, right?'

(80) 个也好着很哩，啦？
kɤ	iɛ	xɔ=tsɤ=xɤ̃		li,	la?
this	also	good=COMP=very		PART	TAG

'This is good too, right?'

The third form of a tag question is "declarative clause, *ʂɤ̃mɤ tsi*?" or "*ʂɤ̃mɤ tsi*, declarative clause?", in which *ʂɤ̃mɤ tsi* is used for asking the reason for the declarative clause and can sometimes be placed before it. For example:

(81) 扎西铺子里没，什么做了？
tsaɕi	phutsi=li	mi,	ʂɤ̃mɤ	tsi=lɔ?
PN	store=LOC	NEG	what	do=PFV

'Zhaxi is not in the store, what is wrong?'

(82) 什么做着个，你饭好好儿不吃？
ʂɤ̃mɤ	tsi=tsɤ	kɤ,	ni	fã	xɔxɤ	pu	tʂhi?
what	do=PROG	PART	2	food	properly	NEG	eat

'What is going on, you are not eating properly?'

7.7 Subordinate clause

7.7.1 Relative clause

A relative clause modifies a head noun. The relativization marker is 的 =tɤ, and a range of components can be relativized in Zhoutun. See the following examples:

(83) 个子大着很的箇一个人来了。
    kɤtsi   ta=tʂɤ=xɤ̃=tɤ   kuɤ   i=kɤ   ʴɤ̃   lɛ=lɔ.
    stature   tall=COMP=very=REL   that   one=CL   person   come=PFV
    'The person who is very tall came.'

(84) 个学生娃看着的书。
    kɤ   ɕyɤsɤ̃ua   khã=tʂɤ=tɤ   fu.
    this   student   read=PROG=REL   book
    'The book this student is reading.'

(85) 我扎西哈给掉的一本书。
    ŋɤ   tʂaɕi=xa   ki=tiɔ=tɤ   i=pɤ̃   fu.
    1   PN=DAT   give=COMP=REL   one=CL   book
    'The book that I gave to Zhaxi.'

(86) 我书一本给掉的箇扎西啊寻着哩。
    ŋɤ   fu   i=pɤ̃   ki=tiɔ=tɤ   kuɤ   tʂaɕi=a   ɕĩ=tʂɤ   li.
    1   book   one=CL   give=COMP=REL   that   PN=ACC   find=PROG   PART
    'I was looking for the Zhaxi to whom I had given a book.'

(87) 书多着很的扎西。
    fu   tuɤ=tʂɤ=xɤ̃=tɤ   tʂaɕi.
    book   many=COMP=very=REL   PN
    'Zhaxi who has a lot of books.'

In (83)–(87), the subject, object, direct object (recipient-like role), indirect object (theme-like role) and genitive are relativized. The complement in a copula clause cannot be relativized. For example:

(88) *扎西 re 的老师。
    *tʂaɕi   ʴi=tɤ   lɔsi.
    PN   COP=REL   teacher
    'Zhaxi, who is a teacher.'

Relative clauses are subject to a pair of restrictions that do not affect independent and main clauses.

First, final particles cannot be used in a relative clause. For example:

(89) a 学生娃书看着个。
    ɕyɹsʅ̃ua   fu   khã=tʂʅ   kʅ.
    student   book   look=PROG   PART
    'Students are reading books.'
 b 书看着（*个）的学生娃。
    fu   khã=tʂʅ   (*kʅ)=tʅ   ɕyɹsʅ̃ua.
    book   look=PROG   (PART)=REL   student
    'The students who are reading books.'

Final particles are very common in main clauses (89a), but they are not allowed in relative clauses (89b).

Second, aspect markers are usually avoided in relative clauses. For example:

(90) a 鸡蛋煮上了。
    tɕitã   tʂu=xã=lɔ.
    egg   boil=COMP=PFV
    'The egg was boiled.'
 b 煮上的鸡蛋。
    tʂu=xã=tʅ   tɕitã.
    boil=COMP=REL   egg
    'The egg that was boiled./The boiled egg.'

The perfective marker $=lɔ$ occurring in the independent clauses (90a) is normally not used in the relative clause in (90b).

The relativization in Zhoutun is schematically summarized in (91):

(91) a Subject: SOV → OV=$tʅ$ S
     b Object: SOV → SV=$tʅ$ O
     c Direct object: $SO_iO_dV → SO_i$=$tʅ$ O_d
     d Indirect object: $SO_iO_dV → SO_d$=$tʅ$ O_i
     e Genitive: N_1= $tʅ$ N_2V → N_2V=$tʅ$ N_1

7.7.2 Complement clause

In Zhoutun, there is no specific complementizer used in complement clauses. This implies that there is no formally distinguishable complement

136 *Clause structure*

clause in Zhoutun. The verb 说 ʂuʏ 'say', for example, may have an object clause, but since no complementizer is found, it is difficult to determine the boundary of the object complement clause. For example:

(92) 冬天到时阿吉学生教哩说。
      tũthiã tɔ   ʂi   atɕi ɕyʏsʏ̃ tɕiɔ li ʂuʏ.
      winter arrive when 3   student teach PART say
    a 'When winter arrives, s/he says that s/he will teach the students.'
    b 'S/he says that when winter arrives s/he will teach students'

Example (92) has two interpretations, depending on whether the expression "when winter arrives" is within the complement clause of the verb ʂuʏ 'say'.

7.7.3 Adverbial clause

Zhoutun uses two multifunctional postpositional markers in adverbial clauses, namely, 时 ʂi, occurring in temporal clauses and conditional clauses, and 呀 ʂa, which can convey adversative, causal, concessive and progressive meanings. Let us see both markers in the following examples:

(93) a 我地啊拖掉时碗洗去哩。
      ŋʏ tshi=a   thuʏ=tiɔ   ʂi   uã   ɕi   tɕhi li.
      1   floor=ACC mop=COMP when bowl wash go PART
      'When I finish mopping the floor, I will go wash the bowls.'
   b 你的钱儿丢掉时，怎嘛做哩？
      ni=tʏ   tɕhie tiu=tiɔ   ʂi,   tʂhima tsi li?
      2=GEN money lost=COMP COND how   do   PART
      'What would you do if you lost your money?'

(94) a 我啊今儿乏着很呀，我饭馆开着哩。
      ŋa tɕie xua=tʂʏ=xʏ̃   ʂa,   ŋʏ fãkuã khɛ=tʂʏ li.
      1:DAT today tired=COMP=very though 1 eatery run=PROG PART
      'Even though I am tired today, I am still running the eatery.'
   b 我啊一天乏着很呀，钱挣着多。
      ŋa i   thiã xua=tʂʏ=xʏ̃   ʂa,   tɕhie tʂʏ̃=tʂʏ=tuʏ.
      1:DAT one day tired=COMP=very because today earn=COMP=much
      'Because I work hard all day, I earn much money.'
   c 早晨天爷下呀，我街上去哩。
      tsɔʂʏ̃   thiãiɛ ɕia ʂa,   ŋʏ kɛ=xã   tɕhi li.
      tomorrow rain fall even_if 1 street=LOC go PART
      'Even if it rains tomorrow, I am going to the street.'

d 夏天是吵，冬天是吵，中午里睡时好说。
   ɕiathiã   ʂi   ʂa,   tũthiã   ʂi   ʂa,
   summer   COP   no_matter   winter   COP   no_matter
   tʂũu=li   ʂui   ʂi   xɔ   ʂuɤ.
   noon=LOC   sleep   COND   good   say
   'It is said that it is good to sleep at noon no matter in summer or in winter.'

It is understandable that a word meaning "time" (e.g., *ʂi*) can grammaticalize into a subordinator "when" and "if", but for *ʂa*, whose original meaning is unclear, it is difficult to explain why it carries out so many functions. Synchronically, *ʂa* appears to be a generic adverbial subordinator, and the various inter-clausal relations it marks are specified by the context.

7.8 Topic structure

There are two topic markers in Zhoutun, namely, 啊 *a* and 么 *mɤ*. Both derive from a final particle, as is typical with Chinese topic markers. For example:

(95) a 水果树啊，嘚就楂，甜梨，酸梨…
      fɿkuɤfu   a   tɤ   tɕiu   ʐuɤ,   thiã   li,   suã   li.
      fruit_tree   TOP   DM   just   pear   sweet   pear   sour   pear
      'As for fruit trees, there are only pears, including sweet pears and sour pears.'
    b 长啊不长，短啊不短嘀箇。
      tʂhã   a   pu   tʂhã,   tuã   a   pu   tuã   ti   kuɤ.
      long   TOP   NEG   long   short TOP   NEG   short   PART   that
      'Long, that is not long; short, that is not short.'

(96) a 三间大房里么亮亮儿有个。
      sã=tɕiã   ta   fã=li   mɤ   liãliɛ   iɔ   kɤ.
      three=CL   big   room=LOC   TOP   bright   have   PART
      'In these three big houses, it is all very bright.'
    b 我的阿妈么针线做着个。
      ŋɤ=tɤ   ama   mɤ   tʂɿ̃ɕiã   tsi=tʂɤ   kɤ.
      1=GEN   mother   TOP   needlework   do=PROG   PART
      'As for my mother, she was doing needlework.'

Li and Thompson (1976) argued that Chinese is a "topic-prominent language". As a Chinese variety, Zhoutun retains this characteristic. This

138　Clause structure

feature is clearly reflected by the use of the identical topic structure[1] as in (113b), which is regarded as "the more characteristic property of topic prominent languages" (Liu 2004: 20).

Note

1 An identical topic (also known as coying topic) is a topic that is fully or partially identical to a corresponding element in the following part of the clause (Liu 2004: 20).

References

Acuo, Yixiweisa, and Xun Xiang. 2015. "Wutunhua de Shengdiao" [The Tones of Wutun]. *Zhongguo Yuwen* [Studies of the Chinese Language] (6): 483–97.
Aikhenvald, Alexandra. 2006. "Serial Verb Constructions in Typological Perspective." In *Serial Verb Constructions: A Cross-Linguistic Typology*, edited by Alexandra Aikhenvald and Robert M. W. Dixon. Oxford: Oxford University Press.
Aikhenvald, Alexandra. 2010. *Imperatives and Commands*. Oxford Studies in Typology and Linguistic Theory. Oxford: Oxford University Press.
Aikhenvald, Alexandra. 2015. *The Art of Grammar: A Practical Guide*. Oxford: Oxford University Press.
Bhat, Darbhe N. Shankara. 1999. *The Prominence of Tense, Aspect and Mood*. Amsterdam: Benjamins.
Bloomfield, Leonard. 1933. *Language*. London: George Allex & Unwin LTD.
Cao, Zhiyun. 2008. *Hanyu Fangyan Dituji* [Linguistic Atlas of Chinese Dialects]. Beijing: The Commercial Press.
Chao, Yuen-Ren. 1930. "ə sistim əv 'toun-letəz' [A system of 'tone-letters']." *Le Maître Phonétique* 30: 24–27.
Clements, George N. 1975. "The Logophoric Pronoun in Ewe: Its Role in Discourse." *Journal of West African Languages* 10: 141–77.
Comrie, Bernard. 1976. *Aspect*. Cambridge: Cambridge University Press.
Crystal, David. 2008. *A Dictionary of Linguistics and Phonetics 6th Edition*. Malden: Blackwell Publishing.
Culy, Christopher. 1997. "Logophoric Pronouns and Point of View." *Linguistics* 35: 845–59.
Dixon, Robert M. W. 2010. *Basic Linguistic Theory. Volume 1: Methodology*. Oxford: Oxford University Press.
Dixon, Robert M.W., and Alexandra Y. Aikhenvald. 2003. "Word: A Typological Framework." In *Word: A Cross-Linguistic Typology*, edited by R. M. W. Dixon and Alexandra Y. Aikhenvald, 1–41. Cambridge: Cambridge University Press.
Dryer, Matthew. 1992. "The Greenbergian Word Order Correlations." *Language* 68 (1): 81–138.
Grant, Anthony P. 2012. "Processes of Grammaticalisation and 'Borrowing the Unborrowable': Contact-Induced Change and the Integration and

Grammaticalisation of Borrowed Terms for Some Core Grammatical Construction Types." In *Grammatical Replication and Borrowability in Language Contact*, edited by Björn Wiemer, Bernhard Wälchi, and Björn Hansen, 191–232. Berlin: De Gruyter Mouton.

Haspelmath, Martin. 2004. "Coordinating Constructions: An Overview." In *Coordinating Constructions*, edited by Martin Haspelmath, 3–39. Amsterdam: John Benjamins.

Heine, Bernd, and Tania Kuteva. 2002. *World Lexicon of Grammaticalization*. Cambridge: Cambridge University Press.

Huang, Yan. 2000. *Anaphora: A Cross-Linguistic Study*. Oxford: Oxford University Press.

Janhunen, Juha, Marja Peltomaa, Erika Sandman, and Xiawu Dongzhou. 2008. *Wutun*. Munich: Lincom Europa.

Kuteva, Tania, Bernd Heine, Bo Hong, Haiping Long, Heiko Narrog, and Seongha Rhee. 2019. *World Lexicon of Grammaticalization*. 2nd ed. Cambridge University Press.

Li, Charles N. 1983. "Languages in Contact in western China." *Papers in East Asian Languages*, 1: 31–51.

Li, Charles N., and Sandra Thompson. 1976. "Subject and Topic: A New Typology of Language." In *Subject and Topic*, edited by Charles Li, 457–89. New York: Academic Press.

Li, Lan, and Hilary M. Chappell. 2013. "Hanyu Fangyan Zhong de Chuzhishi He 'Ba' Ziju [On the Disposal Constructions and Ba Constructions in Chinese Dialects]." *Fangyan* [Dialects] (1): 11–30.

Liu, Danqing. 2004. "Identical Topics: A More Characteristic Property of Topic Prominent Languages." *Journal of Chinese Linguistics* 32 (1): 20–64.

Liu, Danqing. 2008. *Yufa Diaocha Yanjiu Shouce* [A Handbook for Grammatical Investigation and Research]. Shanghai: Shanghai Educational Publishing House.

Liu, Danqing. 2011. "Yuyan Kucang Leixingxue Gouxiang" [Linguistic Inventory Typology: A Proposal for a New Approach to Linguistic Typology]. *Dangdai Yuyanxue* [Contemporary Linguistics] 13 (4): 289–303.

Liu, Danqing. 2012a. "Hanyu de Ruogan Xianhe Fanchou: Yuyan Kucang Leixingxue Shijiao" [Some Mighty Categories in Chinese: A Perspective of Linguistic Inventory Typology]. *Shijie Hanyu Jiaoxue* [Chinese Teaching in The World] 26 (3): 291–305.

Liu, Danqing. 2012b. "Hanyu Chabiju He Huati Jiegou de Tonggouxing" [The Homogeneity of Comparison and Topic Structure in Chinese: An Illustration of the Expansive Power of Mighty Categories]. *Yuyan Yanjiu* [Studies in Languages and Linguistics] 32 (4): 1–12.

Liu, Danqing. 2015. "Hanyu Ji Qinlin Yuyan Liandongshi de Jufa Diwei He Xianhedu" [Syntactic Status and Mightiness of Serical Verb Construction in Chinese and Neighboring Languages]. *Minzu Yuwen* [Minority Languages of China] 3: 3–22.

Malchukov, Andrej L., Martin Haspelmath, and Bernard Comrie. 2010. "Ditransitive Constructions: A Typological Overview." In *Studies in Ditransitive*

Constructions: A Comparative Handbook, edited by Andrej L. Malchukov, Martin Haspelmath, and Bernard Comrie. Berlin: De Gruyter Mouton.
Malchukov, Andrej L., and Heiko Narrog. 2008. "Case Polysemy." In *The Oxford Handbook of Case*, edited by Andrej L. Malchukov and Andrew Spencer, 518–35. Oxford: Oxford University Press.
Mithun, Marianne. 1988. "The Grammaticalization of Coordination." In *Clause Combining in Grammar and Discourse*, edited by John Haiman and Sandra A. Thompson, 331–59. Amsterdam: John Benjamins.
Næss, Åshild. 2008. "Varieties of Dative". In *The Oxford Handbook of Case*, edited by Andrej L. Malchukov and Andrew Spencer, 572–80. Oxford: Oxford University Press.
Nichols, Johanna. 1986. "Head-marking and Depending-marking Grammar." *Language* 62 (1): 56–119.
Palmer, F. R. 2001. *Mood and Modality*. 2nd ed. Cambridge: Cambridge University Press.
Ren, Bisheng. 2006. *Qinghai Fangyan Yufa Zhuanti Yanjiu* [A Special Study on the Grammar of Qinghai Dialect]. Xining: Qinghai People's Publishing House.
Sandman, Erika. 2016. "A Grammar of Wutun." PhD diss., University of Helsinki, Helsinki.
Schachter, Paul, and Timothy Shopen. 2007. "Parts-of Speech Systems." In *Language Typology and Syntactic Description. Volume 1: Clause Structure*, edited by Timothy Shopen, 2nd ed., 1–60. Cambridge: Cambridge University Press.
Slater, Keith. 2003. *A Grammar of Mangghuer: A Mongolic Language of China's Qinghai-Gansu Sprachbund*. London: Routledge Curzon.
Thomason, Sarah Grey, and Terrence Kaufman. 1988. *Language Contact, Creolization, and Genetic Linguisitcs*. Berkeley: University of California Press.
Xu, Dan. 2014. *Tangwanghua Yanjiu* [Studies on Tangwang]. Beijing: The Ethnic Publishing House.
Xu, Dan, and Qibin Ran. 2020. *Gansu Dongxiang Tangwanghua* [The Description of Tangwang in Dongxiang, Gansu]. Beijing: The Commercial Press.
Zhang, Bojiang. 1997. "Xingzhi xingrongci de fanwei he cengci" [Scope and Level of Qualitative Adjectives]. *Yufa Yanjiu he Tansuo* [Grammar Research and Exploration] 8: 50–61.
Zhe, Wankui. 2001. *Zhoutun de Lishi* [The History of Zhoutun]. Mimeographed booklet.
Zhou, Chenlei. 2016. "Cong Hanyu Fangyan Beidongju Shishi Bixian Kan Xingshi Kucang Dui Yuyi Fanchou de Zhiyue" [On the Restriction of Form and Meaning from the Perspective of Agent in Passive in Chinese Dialects]. *Yuyan Yanjiu* [Studies in Languages and Linguistics] 36 (1): 59–66.
Zhou, Chenlei. 2017. "On the Word Order of Ditransitive Constructions in Northwestern Chinese." *Journal of China Studies* 20 (3): 29–45.
Zhou, Chenlei. 2019a. "A Special Case Marking System in the Sinitic Languages of Northwest China." *Journal of Chinese Linguistics* 47 (2): 425–52.
Zhou, Chenlei. 2019b. "Ganqing fangyan gebiaoji *ha* de laiyuan" [The Origin of the Dative-Accusative Marker *xa* in Gan-Qing Dialects]. *Language and Linguistics* 20 (3): 493–513.

Zhou, Chenlei. 2020a. "Case Markers and Language Contact in the Gansu-Qinghai Linguistic Area." *Asian Languages and Linguistics* 1 (1): 168–203.
Zhou, Chenlei. 2020b. "The Structure of Num+CL in the Zhōutún Dialect: Issues Induced by Language Contact." *Language and Linguistics* 21 (1): 145–73.
Zhou, Chenlei. 2021. "On the Disjunctive Constructions and Related Constructions in Zhoutun." *Lingua*. https://doi.org/10.1016/j.lingua.2021.103183.
Zhou, Chenlei. 2022. "From 'Two' to a Comitative-Instrumental Case Marker: A Regional Innovation in the Gansu-Qinghai Linguistic Area." *Language and Linguistics* 23(2), 349–369. https://doi.org/10.1075/lali.00109.zho.

Appendices

I. Text "The past life in Zhoutun"

我们尕尕有时，喏的现在的般这么灯泡儿没嘛。

ŋʐ=mʐ	kaka	iu	ɕi,	tʐ=tʐ	ɕiãtsɛ=tʐ	pã	tʂʐmʐ
1=PL	little	have	when	now=GEN	now=GEN	POST	this_way

t̃ʐ̃phʐ	mɨ	ma,
bulb	NEG	PART

'When we were young, there were no light bulbs like the bulbs in today.'

灯盏儿么喏，我记得时，泥兰捏上了着，圆圆儿这么捏上，窝窝儿个挖上时筒里。

t̃ʐ̃tsʐ	mʐ	tʐ,	ŋʐ tɕite	ɕi,	mi=lã	niɛ=xã=lɔ=tʂʐ,
oil_lamp	TOP	DM	1 remember	when	mud=INS	pinch=COMP=PFV=PROG

yãyʐ	tʂʐmʐ	niɛ=xã,	uʐuʐ=kʐ	ua=xã	ɕi	kuʐli.
roundly	this_way	pinch=COMP	hole=CL	dig=COMP	when	there

'I remember that the lamps were made of clay, so (they were) round and pinched, and a nest was dug in the top, into which clear oil was poured.'

清油啊倒给时，捻子说着，棉花啊着上了时，煤油里杵给了着。

tɕhiu=a	tɔ=ki	ɕi,	niãtsi u=tʂʐ,	miãxua=a	tshuʐ=xã=lɔ
oil=ACC	pour=VIM	when	spill say=PROG	cotton=ACC	fire=COMP=PFV

ɕi,	miiu=li	tʂhu=ki=lɔ=tʂʐ.
when	oil=LOC	stand=VIM=PFV=PROG

'When clear oil was poured, we lit the cotton that is used to make the spill and put it into the oil.'

蘸着湿湿了给时，喏，烟叶上打上了着，洋火兰。

tʂã=tʂʐ	ɕiɕi=lɔ=ki	ɕi,	tʐ,	iãiɛ=xã	ta=xã=lɔ=tʂʐ,
dip=PROG	wet=PFV=VIM	when	DM	tobacco=LOC	light=COMP=PFV=PROG

iãxuɤ=lã.
match=INS
'Dipped wet, it was fired through the tobacco with a match.'

嗻打火机没呗，洋火兰个点着了着，着给了着。
tɤ taxuɤtɕi mɿ pi, iãxuɤ=lã kɤ tiã=tʂuɤ=lɔ=tʂɤ,
DM lighter NEG PART match=INS this light=COMP=PFV=PROG
tʂuɤ=ki=lɔ=tʂɤ.
light=VIM=PFV=PROG
'In those days there was no lighter, so matches were used to light it.'

着着完了去了，靠棍棍儿兰往上点儿拨给。
tʂuɤ=tʂɤ=uã=lɔ tɕhi=lɔ, khɔ kũkũ=lã uã ʂã tiɛ puɤ=ki.
light=PROG=finish=PFV go=PFV again stick=INS towards up little fiddle=VIM
'After it was lit, it burned away and then a small stick was used to poke it upward.'

这么时，三间大房里么亮亮儿有个。
tʂɤmɤ ʂi, sã=tɕiã ta fã=li mɤ liãliɛ iɔ kɤ.
this_way when three=CL big room=LOC TOP bright have PART
'By doing that, the three large houses were lit up.'

后头后头后头嗻，清油的灯盏儿趴奄下了着，
xuɤthu xuɤthu xuɤthu tɤ, tɕhĩiu=tɤ tɤ̃tʂɤ pata=xɤ=lɔ=tʂɤ,
after after after DM oil=GEN oil_lamp droop=COMP=PFV=PROG
'After a while, the lamp with clear oil was lying down.'

洋油的灯盏儿。清油洋油照哩照哩嗻，煤油，
iãiu=tɤ tɤ̃tʂɤ. tɕhĩiu iãiu tʂɔ li tʂɔ li tɤ, mɿiu
oil=GEN oil_lamp oil oil light PART light PART DM kerosene
'The lamps with clear oil and foreign oil¹ were always used, but later they were replaced by kerosene ones.'

合作社里煤油倒上时，来时，煤油的灯盏儿越点儿亮哩。
xuɤtsuɤʂɤ=li mɿiu tɔ=xã ʂi lɛ ʂi, mɿiu=tɤ
cooperative=LOC kerosene pour=COMP when come when kerosene=GEN
tɤ̃tʂɤ yɤ tiɛ liã li.
lamp more little bright PART
'You can get some kerosene from the cooperative, and the kerosene lamps were brighter.'

煤油完上时，原清油灯盏儿照着嘀，
miiu   uã=xã   ʂi,   yã   tɕhĩu   tr̃tʂɤ   tsɔ=tʂɤ   ti,
kerosene finish=COMP when again oil   lamp   light=PROG PART
'When the kerosene ran out, the clear oil lamps were used again for lighting.'

就这么生活过着。后头嘚电拉上了着，时代变了，电么拉上了。
tɕiu   tsɤmɤ   sr̃xur   kuɤ=tʂɤ.   xuthu   tɤ   tiã
just   this_way   life   live=PROG after   DM   electricity
la=xã=lɔ=tʂɤ,   site piã=lɔ,   tiã   mɤ la=xã=lɔ=tʂɤ.
build=COMP=PFV=PROG time change=PFV electricity TOP build=COMP=PFV=PROG
'That was how life went on. Then came electricity, and the times changed with electricity.'

电么拉上时嘚亮着，绕的个 re 最前。
tiã   mɤ la=xã   ʂi   tɤ liã=tʂɤ,   ɟɔ=tɤ
electricity TOP build=COMP when DM bright=PROG dazzling=NOMZ
kɤ   ɟi,   tsui   tɕhiã.
PART COP   most   front
'It was bright when electricity was introduced, and it was blindingly bright at first.'

灯啊着给时，灯泡儿着给时，绕着看不下哩，亮着。
tr̃=a   tsuɤ=ki   ʂi,   tr̃phɤ tsuɤ=ki   ʂi,   ɟɔ=tʂɤ
bulb=ACC light=VIM   when bulb   light=VIM when dazzling=PROG
khã=pu=xa   li,   liã=tʂɤ.
look=NEG=COMP   PART   bright=PROG
'When the lights were on, the bulbs lit up so brightly that your eyes stung, and you couldn't see.'

嘚煤油的箇灯盏儿么，清油的灯盏儿么，乌拉乌头这么有哩呗。
tɤ   miiu=tɤ   tr̃tʂɤ mɤ,   tɕhĩu=tɤ   tr̃tʂɤ mɤ,
DM   kerosene=GEN   lamp   TOP   oil=GEN   lamp   TOP
ulauthu   tsɤmɤ   iu   li   pi.
dark   this_way   exist   PART   PART
'Kerosene lamps and clear oil lamps are both dark (comparatively).'

我的阿妈么尽晚夕里到时，灯盏儿擦，针线做着个，针么穿上着没哩，黑了着不见哩，我们啊穿给说着。
ŋɤ=tɤ   ama   mɤ   tei   uãɕi=li   tɔ   ʂi,   tr̃tʂɤ   tsha,
1=GEN   mother TOP all   night=LOC   arrive   when   lamp   wipe

```
tʂɤ̃ɕiã        tsi=tʂɤ     kɤ,     tʂɤ̃      mɤ     tʂhuã=xã=tʂɤ         mɨ    li,
needlework    do=PROG    PART    neelde    TOP    thread=COMP=PROG    NEG   PART
xi=lɔ=tʂɤ             pu      tɕiã    li,     ŋɤ=mɤ=a         tʂhuã=kɨ       u=tʂɤ.
dark=PFV=PROG         NEG     see     PART    1=PL=DAT        thread=VIM     say=PROG
```
'My mother wiped the lamps at night and did needlework. When the needle could not be threaded and it was too dark to see, she let us thread the needle.'

针啊穿时，我们也尕嘛，眼睛吵亮点儿啁，当下穿不上哩，就这么有个呀。
```
tʂɤ=a           tʂhuã    si,      ŋɤ=mɤ    iɛ      ka       ma,       niãtɕi    ʂa
needle=ACC      thread   when     1=CL     also    young    PART      eye       though
liã             tiɛ      tɤ,      tãɕia    tʂhuã=pu=xã             li,       tɕiu
bright          little   DM       then     thread=NEG=COMP         PART      just
tʂɤmɤ                   iɔ       kɤ       ia.
this_way                have     PART     PART
```
'We were young when we were threading the needle, and although our eyes were better than Mom's, we couldn't put it on. That's what happened.'

一点儿燃时，还点儿油点儿掺的箇个，不掺时完下了着，灭下哩呀，哦了。
```
itiɛ         ɻã       ʂi,      xã       tiɛ      iu      tiɛ      tʂhã=tɤ         kuɤ     kɤ,
little       fire     when     also     little   oil     little   add=NOMZ        that    PART
pu           tʂhã     ʂi       uã=xɤ=lɔ=tʂɤ,           miɛ=xɤ          li    ia,     ɔlɤ.
NEG          add      COND     finish=COMP=PFV=PROG    out=COMP        PART  PART    over
```
'After burning for a while, we had to add some oil, and if we didn't add oil, it would go out after burning.'

啁中的个，箇巴里时呐这么的一坨坨亮着时，啁灯般有哩呗啁说时，
```
tɤ      tʂũ      tɤkɤ,     kuɤ      pa=li       ʂina     tʂɤmɤ=tɤ            ithuɤthuɤ
DM      good     PART      that     time=LOC    time     this_way=NOMZ       little
liã=tʂɤ                  ʂi,      tɤ      tɤ̃      pã       iu      li      pɨ       tɤ
bright=PROG              when     DM      lamp    POST     exist   PART    PART     DM
ʂuɤ                     ʂi,
say                     COND
```
'Now it's better. At that time, there was so little bright, and now there are lamps,'

灯盏儿有哩呗。啁现在越亮时越还亮点儿，看哩嘛，
```
tɤ̃tʂɤ         iu       li       pɨ.      tɤ      ɕiãtsɛ      yuɤ       liã        ʂi
lamp          exist    PART     PART     DM      now         more      bright     COND
```

yuʁ xã tiɛ liã, khã li ma,
more also little bright see PART PART
'There are lamps, and now it is getting brighter and brighter.'

一晚夕么电没时心急着很的，啦？
i uãɕi mʁ tiã mɨ ʂi ɕĩ tɕi=tʂʁ=xɽ̃ tʁ, la?
one night TOP electricity NEG COND heart anxious=PROG=very PART TAG
'If you don't have electricity at night, you get very anxious, don't you?'

书看时嘚瓶瓶儿，罐头瓶瓶儿，罐头箇有个，
fu khã ʂi tʁ phĭphiɛ, kuãthu phĭphiɛ kuãthu kuʁ
book read when DM bottle can bottle can that
iɔ kʁ,
have PART
'When reading books, you take a bottle, or a canning jar'

嘚这么的盐水瓶瓶儿上么，扣下里么，光仰碗么啊扣下了着，碗的底底里么也油倒上了着，
tʁ tʂʁmʁ=tʁ iãfi phĭphiɛ=xã mʁ, khu=xʁ li
DM this_way=NOMZ brine bottle=LOC TOP invert=COMP PART
mʁ, kuã iã uã=ma khu=xʁ=lɔ=tʂʁ,
TOP only also bowl=PL:ACC invert=COMP=PFV=PROG
uã=tʁ tsitsi=li mʁ iɛ iu tɔ=xã=lɔ=tʂʁ,
bowl=GEN bottom=LOC TOP also oil pour=COMP=PFV=PROG
'or a bottle containing salt water, and put it upside down; you take a bowl and put it upside down, you pour oil in the bottom of the bowl,'

也灯泡儿照着个，嘚就书看哩说时，
iɛ tɽ̃phʁ tʂɔ=tʂʁ kʁ, tʁ tɕiu fu khã li ʂuʁ ʂi,
also bulb glare=PROG PART DM just book read PART say when
'You fire it to make it shining like a light bulb, then you can read.'

灯盏儿啊底底里拿了下来了，书的跟前儿瞧的个么看的箇个，
tɽ̃tʂʁ=a tsitsi=li na=lɔ xalɛ=lɔ, fu=tʁ kɽ̃tɕhiɛ tɕhiɔ=tʁ
lamp=ACC bottom=LOC take=PFV down=PFV book=GEN near read=NOMZ
kʁ mʁ khã=tʁ kuʁ kʁ,
PART TOP read=NOMZ that PART
'You take the lamp down from the bottom of the bowl and bring it to the heel of the book to read.'

不看时不见哩，字列。坐着远时不见哩。
pu khã ʂi pu tɕiã li, tsi=liɛ, tsuʁ=tʂʁ=yã
NEG read COND NEG see PART word=CL sit=COMP=far

ʂi		pu		tɕiã	li.		
COND		NEG		see	PART		

'If you do not use the lamp to read, you will not see any words. You can't see the words if you sit far away.'

箇，瓶瓶儿么个寻见时，
kuʐ,	phĩphiɛ	mʐ	kʐ	ɕĩ=tɕiã		ʂi,
that	bottle	TOP	CL	search=COMP		COND

'If you find a bottle,'

扣了摆下着，箇的底底上的灯盏儿个放给时，
khu=lɔ	liɔ=xʐ=tʂʐ,	kuʐ=tʐ	tsitsi=xã=tʐ	tĩtʂʐ=kʐ
invert=PFV	throw=COMP=PROG	that=GEN	bottom=LOC=GEN	lamp=CL

fã=kɨ	ʂi,			
put=VIM	COND			

'You put it upside down, and put a lamp at the bottom of the bottle,'

点儿高呗，高时书啊底底里拿了看时嘚见的个 re。
tiɛ	kɔ	pɨ,	kɔ	ʂi	fu=a	tsitsi=li	na=lɔ	khã
little	high	PART	high	COND	book=ACC	bottom=LOC	take=PFV	read

ʂi	tʐ	tɕiã=tʐ	kʐ	ɖi.
COND	DM	see=NOMZ	PART	COP

'The lamp is a little high. If it is high, you put the book under the lamp, and you can see it.'

孽障哩，箇巴里点儿生活困难，
niɛtʂã	li.	kuʐ	pa=li	tiɛ	sĩxuʐ	khũnã,
pitiful	PART	that	time=LOC	little	life	tough

'What a pity life! Life was very difficult in the past. It was difficult at that time.'

钱么的个拿了着嘚没哩。出去时，钱没嘛，
tɕhiã	mʐ	tʐ	kʐ	na=lɔ=tʂʐ	tʐ	mɨ	li.	tʂhutɕhi
money	TOP	DM	this	take=PFV=PROG	DM	NEG	PART	go_out

ʂi,	tɕhiã	mɨ	ma,					
when	money	NEG	PART					

'Once you took some money, they were gone soon. When you go out, there was no money on you.'

几分几分嘛，一分二分兰走着嘛。
tɕi fɤ̃ tɕi fɤ̃ ma, i fɤ̃ ɤ fɤ̃=lã tsɯ=tʂɤ ma,
few cent few cent PART one cent two cent=COM walk=PROG PART
'A few cents, just a cent or two cents to take with you to go.'

二分钱儿给时，糖哈买去时，两个么给的给，高兴着。
ɤ   fɤ̃   tɕhiɛ   ki,   ʂi,   thã=xa   mɛ   tɕhi   ʂi,
two cent money give COND candy=ACC buy   go   COND
liã=kɤ   mɤ   ki=tɤ   ki,   kɔɕĩ=tʂɤ,
two=CL TOP give=NOMZ give happy=PROG
'If you are given two cents, you could go buy candy. You could buy two pieces of candy. You felt very happy.'

旋学旋学嘚一毛么给着哩呗。
ɕyã̠ɕyɤɕyã̠ɕyɤ   tɤ   i   mɔ   mɤ   ki=tʂɤ   li,   pi.
thereafter   DM one dime TOP give=PROG PART PART
'Further on, you will be given ten cents.'

嘚现在的尕娃娃嘛，一毛阿里要哩，五毛给时，"屁哩呀"这么说的个re。
tɤ   ɕiãtsɛ=tɤ   ka   uaua   ma,   i   mɔ   ali   iɔ
DM now=GEN   little child PART one dime where want
li,   u   mɔ   ki   ʂi,   phi   li   ia   tʂɤmɤ
PART five dime give when nonsense PART PART this_way
ʂuɤ=tɤ   kɤ   ɖi.
say=NOMZ PART COP
'Nowadays, who wants a dime? If you give a child 50 cents, they will say "shit."'

箇巴里是时，周屯三十个人有哩么？
kuɤpa=li   ʂi   ʂi   tʂuthũ   sã̠ʂi=kɤ   ɖɤ̃   iuu   li   mɤ?
that_time=LOC COP when Zhoutun thirty=CL people exist PART Q
'In the old days, were there 30 people in Zhoutun?'

几家人，七家人么是？七家嘛时这么的个说着哩嘛。
tɕi   tɕia   ɖɤ̃,   tɕhi   tɕia   ɖɤ̃   mɤ   ʂi?
several   family   people seven family   people   Q   COP
tɕhi   tɕia   ma   ʂi   tʂɤmɤ=tɤ   kɤ   ʂuɤ=tʂɤ   li   ma.
seven family PART when this_way=NOMZ this say=PROG PART PART
'How many families were there, seven? Seven, I think.'

箇巴里，以前，周屯里就坐下时人。
kuɤpa=li,   itɕhiã,   tsuthũ=li   tɕiu   tsuɤ=xɤ   ɕi   tɤ̃.
that_time=LOC before   Zhoutun=LOC just   live=COMP when   people
'In the past, there were people living in Zhoutun.'

箇巴里时，个玉林的阿奶么不是。
kuɤpa=li,   ɕi,   kɤ   ylĩ=tɤ   anɛ   mɤ   pu   ɕi.
that_time=LOC when   this   PN=GEN   grandmother   TOP   NEG   COP
'In the past, not in the days of Yulin's grandmother (before she was born).'

没，还。我们的阿爷，公公么也没，公公的阿大么。
mi,   xã.   ŋɤ=mɤ=tɤ   aiɛ,   kũkũ=mɤ   iɛ   mi,
NEG   still 1=CL=GEN   grandfather grandfather-in-law=TOP   also   NEG
kũkũ=tɤ   ata=mɤ.
grandfather-in-law=GEN   father=TOP
'Our grandfather and grandfather-in-law weren't born yet either. I think it was the time of the generation of my grandfather-in-law's father.'

周屯里，周屯里箇巴里是的吧，
tsuthũ=li,   tsuthũ=li   kuɤpa=li   ɕi   tɤ   pa,
Zhoutun=LOC   Zhoutun=LOC   that_time=LOC COP   PART   PART
'They used to live in Zhoutun.'

一个换集的，一个前庄的。
i=kɤ   xuãtɕi=tɤ,   i=kɤ   tɕhiãtʂuã=tɤ.
one=CL   Huanji (PN)=GEN   one=CL   Qianzhuang (PN)=GEN
'One was from Huanji and the other was from Qianzhuang.'

夏河时就伯伯的老家的名字，嘚还叫着哩，夏河里去呀。
xaxɤ   ɕi   tɕiu   papa=tɤ   lɔtɕia=tɤ   mĩtsi, tɤ   xã
Xiahe (PN)   COND   just   uncle=GEN   hometown=GEN   name   DM   still
tɕiɔ=tʂɤ   li,   xaxɤ=li   tɕhi   ia.
call=PROG   PART   Xiahe=LOC   go   PART
'Your uncle's hometown was called Xiahe, and it is still called that way, such as "Go to Xiahe."'

老前辈么坐下的，夏河叫着个呀。
lɔtɕhiãpi=mɤ   tsuɤ=xɤ   tɤ,   xaxɤ   tɕiɔ=tʂɤ   kɤ   ia.
ancestor=PL   live=COMP   PART   Xiahe   call=PROG   PART   PART
'When our ancestors lived here, it was called Xiahe.'

嗯还夏河叫着哩，周屯的箇人家哈夏河叫着哩。
tʐ   xã   xaxʀ   tɕiɔ=tʂʀ li,   tʂuthũ=tʐ   kuʁ   ɭʐ̃tɕia=xa
DM still Xiahe   call=PROG PART Zhoutun=GEN   that household=ACC
xaxʀ   tɕiɔ=tʂʀ   li.
Xiahe   call=PROG   PART
'It's still called Xiahe. The place where the people in Zhoutun live is called Xiahe.'

夏河时就伯伯的老家，伯伯么夏河的人 re 呀。
xaxʀ   ɕi   tɕiu   papa=tʐ   lɔtɕia,   papa   mʀ   xaxʀ=tʐ
Xiahe   COND   just   uncle=GEN hometown   uncle   TOP   Xiahe=GEN
ɭʐ̃   ɭɨ   ia.
people   COP   PART
'Xiahe is your uncle's hometown. Your uncle's family is from Xiahe.'

上原，下原，还什么叫着嘀，换集的，上换集，下换集，就这么。
ʂãyã,   xayã,   xã   ʂʀ̃mʀ   tɕiɔ=tʂʀ   ti,   xuãtɕi
Shangyuan (PN) Xiayuan (PN) still   what   call=PROG PART   Huanji (PN)
tʐ,   ʂãxuãtɕi,   xaxuãtɕi,   tɕiu   tʂʀmʀ.
PART   Shanghuanji   Xiahuanji   just   this_way
'Shangyuan, Xiayuan, and what's the name, Huanji. Shanghuanji, Xiahuanji.'

个列是嘀周屯里最前来下的。
kʀ   liɛ   ɕi   tʐ   tʂuthũ=li   tsui   tɕhiã   lɛ=xʀ   tʐ.
this   all   COP   DM   Zhoutun=LOC   most   early   come=COMP   PART
'These were the first to come to Zhoutun.'

刚几家人，三十几家嘛，三十几个人说哩嘛时。
tɕiã   tɕi   tɕia   ɭʐ̃,   ʂãʂi   tɕi   tɕia   ma,
only   few   family   people   thirty   several   family   PART
ʂãʂi   tɕi=kʀ   ɭʐ̃   u   li   ma   ɕi.
thirty   few=CL   people   say   PART   PART   COND
'There were only a few families, thirty or so families, (no!) thirty or so people.'

个哈爸爸问的知道哩。
kʀ=xa   papa   uʐ̃   tʐ   tʂitɔ   li.
this=ACC   uncle   ask   PART   know   PART
'Ask your uncle about this. He knows.'

我们的公公的。我也不知道喔，好好儿，
ŋɤ=mɤ=tɤ kũkũ=tɤ.   ŋɤ iɛ   pu tɕitɔ uɤ, xɔxɤ,
1=CL=GEN grandfather=GEN 1 also NEG know PART good_manner
'I don't know much about the origins of our father-in-law's family.'

箇巴里我的公公的阿奶么是哩吧，
kuɤ pa=li   ŋɤ=tɤ kũkũ=tɤ   anɛ=mɤ   ɕi   li   pa.
that time=LOC 1=GEN father=GEN   grandmother=TOP COP PART PART
'In the past, my grandfather's grandmother, grandmother's grandmother, four generations, five generations of people.'

阿奶们的阿奶，四辈人，五辈人。五辈人过了吧，
anɛ=mɤ=tɤ   anɛ,   si   pi   ɻĩ,   u   pi
grandmother=PL=GEN   grandmother four generation people five generation
ɻĩ.   u   pi   ɻĩ,   kuɤ=lɔ   pa,
people   five generation people   pass=PFV PART
'Grandmothers' grandmother, four or five generations, or more than five generations.'

阿爷，箇，阿爷么一辈，我么一辈，扎西么一辈，
aiɛ,   kuɤ, aiɛ=mɤ   i   pi,   ŋɤ=mɤ i   pi,
grandfather that grandfather=CL   one generation   1=CL   one generation
tɕaɕi=mɤ   i   pi,
PN=TOP   one generation
'Grandfather is one generation. I am one generation. Zhaxi is another generation,'

旭旭么一辈，四辈了啊。六辈么七辈人了有个。
ɕyɕy=mɤ   i   pi,   si   pi=lɔ   a,   liu pi
PN=TOP   one generation four generation=PFV   PART six generation
mɤ   tɕhi   pi   ɻĩ=lɔ   have   kɤ,
DISJ   seven   generation people=PFV   exist PART
'Xuxu is a generation. These are already four generations. (Totally) there are six or seven generations.'

嗯个是哩么？个是时嗯，大婆，小婆娶上了个。
tɤ   kɤ   ɕi   li   mɤ?   kɤ   ɕi   ɕi   tɤ,
DM   this COP   PART Q   this COP   COND   DM
taphɤ   ɕiɔphɤ   tɕhy=xã=lɔ   kɤ.
first_wife   youngest_wife   marry=COMP=PFV   PART
'For a certain generation of ancestors, they married a number of wives (first wife and second wife).'

大婆小婆你知道呗。富人家电视里面也大奶奶、二奶奶。
tɑphʏ   ɕiɔphʏ   ni tʂitɔ pɨ.   fu   tʂĩ   tɕiɑ   tiɑ̃si
first_wife youngest_wife 2 know PART rich people family television
limiɑ̃   iɛ   tɑnɛnɛ,   ʏnɛnɛ.
inside   also first_wife second_wife
'You know "tɑphʏ" and "ɕiɔphʏ", right? They are the first and second wife of the rich family in TV dramas.'

嗯嗯，大婆、二婆。还有个，相片。
ʏ̃   ʏ̃   tɑphʏ,   ʏphʏ.   xɑ̃   iɔ   kʏ,   ɕiɑ̃phiɑ̃.
PART PART first_wife second_wife still have PART   photo
'There are also photos of the first wife and the second wife.'

还有哩，阿奶前，我们的，我的婆家里，
xɑ̃ iu   li,   ɑnɛ   tɕhiɑ̃, ŋʏ=mʏ=tʏ, ŋʏ=tʏ phʏtɕhiɑ=li,
still exist PART grandmother POST   1=PL=PN   1=GEN husband_family=LOC
'The photos are still there, in the grandmother's house, my husband's family's house.'

扎西的阿奶前还有哩。
tʂɑɕi=tʏ   ɑnɛ   tɕhiɑ̃   xɑ̃   iu   li.
PN=GEN   grandmother   POST   still eixst   PART
'The photos are in Zhaxi's grandmother's house.'

你没见。相照下了着撒，我哈取上了去时，筒，
ni   mɨ   tɕiɑ̃.   ɕiɑ̃   tʂɔ=xʏ=lɔ=tʂʏ   sɑ,   ŋʏ=xɑ
2   NEG   see   photo   take=COMP=PFV=PROG   PART   1=DAT
tɕhy=xɑ̃=lɔ   tɕhi   ɕi,   kuʏ,
take=COMP=PFV   go   when   that
'You haven't seen them. I was asked to take the photos away,'

年到时头磕，纸烧着么做时，嗯我问了，没知道着，什么是哩喧？
niɑ̃   tɔ   ɕi   thu   khuʏ,   tʂi   sɔ=tʂʏ   mʏ tsi
year arrive when   head   kowtow joss_paper   burn=PROG   Q   do
ɕi,   tʏ   ŋʏ   uʏ=lɔ,   mɨ   tʂitɔ=tʂʏ,   ɕʏ̃mʏ   ɕi   li   xuɑ̃?
when   DM   1   ask=PFV   NEG   know=PROG   what   COP   PART PART
'And when it came time for New Year, you had to kowtow to the photo, burn joss paper, and so on. Then I asked, what is it? I don't know.'

阿爷的画子里还阿奶两个有个说着,
aiɛ=tʁ　　　　xuatsi=li xã anɛ　　liã=kʁ iu kʁ ʂuʁ=tʂʁ,
grandfather=GEN photo=LOC still grandmother two=CL exist PART say=PROG
'There are two grandmothers in the photo of grandfather.'

问了时,个大阿奶,个尕阿奶。
uʁ̃=lɔ　 ɕi,　kʁ　ta　 anɛ,　　 kʁ　 ka　 anɛ.
ask=PFV when this big grandmother this little grandmother
'When I asked him, he said this is the first grandmother and this is the second grandmother.'

大阿奶的后头的列的扎西的太爷,阿爷,
ta anɛ=tʁ　　　　xuthu=tʁ=liɛ=tʁ　tʂaɕi=tʁ theiɛ,　　aiɛ,
big grandmother=GEN after=GEN=CL=GEN PN=GEN great_grandfather grandfather
'After the first grandmother there is Zhaxi's great grandfather and grandfather.'

噎,就这么来了个呀。
tʁ,　 tɕiu　　 tʂʁmʁ　　 lɛ=lɔ　　　 kʁ　　 ia.
DM　 just　　 this_way　 come=PFV　 PART　 PART
'They just came here (in Zhoutun).'

噎我详细好好儿不知道嘛,照片还有个。
tʁ　ŋʁ　ɕiãɕi　xɔxʁ　　　　pu　tʂitɔ　ma,　tʂɔphiã xã　iɔ　 kʁ.
DM　1　detail　good_manner　NEG　know　PART　photos　still have　PART
'I'm not sure about the details, but the photos are still here.'

箇们箇巴里的情况好嘀,噎说时富农 re。
kuʁ=mʁ　kuʁ　pa=li=tʁ　　　　tɕhĩkhuã　xɔ　　 ti　　 tʁ　 ʂuʁ　ɕi
3=PL　that　time=LOC=GEN　situation　good　PART　DM　say　COND
funũ　　　　　ɖi.
rich_peasant　COP
'They were in a good situation: they were called rich farmers.'

河州,我的娘家的阿奶,甘肃河州人是哩说哩。
xuʁtʂu,　　 ŋʁ=tʁ　niãtɕia=tʁ　　　　 anɛ,　 kãsu　 xuʁtʂu
Hezhou (PN)　1=GEN mother's_family=GEN grandmother Gansu (PN) Hezhou
ɖʁ̃　　　 ɕi　　 li　　　 u　　 li.
people　COP　PART　say　PART
'I heard that my mother's grandmother was from Hezhou in Gansu.'

十三岁上我的阿奶来了着。

ʂisã	sui=xã	ŋɤ=tɤ	anɛ	lɛ=lɔ=tʂɤ.
thirteen	year=LOC	1=GEN	grandmother	come=PFV=PROG

'When she was 13 years old, my grandmother came to Zhoutun.'

嘚就马步芳，马步芳说着，嘚箇巴里，土匪，仗打着。马步芳仗打着，阿奶哈没办法着，个儿来了着，呆下了。

tɤ	tɕiu	mapufã,	mapufã	ʂuɤ=tʂɤ,	tɤ	kuɤpa=li,	thufi,
DM	just	PN	PN	say=PROG	DM	that_time=LOC	bandit

tʂã	ta=tʂɤ,	mapufã	tʂã	ta=tʂɤ,	anɛ=xa		mɔ
battle	fight=PROG	PN	battle	fight=PROG	grandmother=DAT		NEG

pãfa=tʂɤ,	kɤ	lɛ=lɔ=tʂɤ,	tɛ=xɤ=lɔ.	
method=PROG	here	come=PFV=PROG	stay=COMP=PFV	

'At that time, the battle against the bandit Bufang Ma² occurred, so she had no choice but to come and live here.'

呆下了嘚婆家个儿给掉了，

tɛ=xɤ=lɔ	tɤ	phɤtɕia	kɤ	ki=tiɔ=lɔ,
stay=COMP=PFV	DM	husband's_family	here	give=COMP=PFV

'After she lived here, she got married.'

阿奶姓什么是不知道说哩，我的阿奶，姓什么是着不知道着，嘚婆家人啊随上了着，

anɛ	ɕĩ	ʂɤ̃mɤ	ʂi	pu	tɕitɔ	u	li,	ŋɤ=tɤ
grandmother	surname	what	COP	NEG	know	say	PART	1=GEN

anɛ,	ɕĩ	ʂɤ̃mɤ	ʂi=tʂɤ	pu	tɕitɔ=tʂɤ,	tɤ
grandmother	surname	what	COP=PROG	NEG	know=PROG	DM

phɤtɕia	.tɤ̃=a	sui=xã=lɔ=tʂɤ.	
husband's_family	people=ACC	follow=COMP=PFV=PROG	

'I don't know my grandmother's surname, but she took her in-laws' surname.'

胡媛姐叫着个，我的阿奶，咃十三岁上给了，

xuyã	tɕiɛ	tɕiɔ=tʂɤ	kɤ,	ŋɤ=tɤ	anɛ,	tha	ʂisã
PN	sister	call=PROG	PART	1=GEN	grandmother	LRP	thirteen

sui=xã	ki=lɔ,						
year=LOC	give=PFV						

'They called her "Sister Hu Yuan". My grandmother said she was given to her in-laws when she was 13 years old,'

长期说着哩呗，一当年儿说的给呀，我啊十三岁上给下了嘀。
tʂhãtɕhi   suɤ=tʂɤ   li   pi,   itãniɛ   suɤ=tɤ=ki   ia   ŋa
long-term say=PROG PART PART always say=NOMZ=VIM PART 1:ACC
ʂisã   sui=xã   ki=xɤ=lɔ   ti.
thirteen   year=LOC   give=COMP=PFV   PART

'For a long period of time, she always told people that she was given to her in-laws when she was 13 years old'

箇巴里，土匪反了着，个儿呆下了着。
kuɤpa=li,   thufi   fã=lɔ=tʂɤ,   kɤ   tɛ=xɤ=lɔ=tʂɤ.
that_time=LOC bandit resist=PFV=PROG   here   stay=COMP=PFV=PROG

'And that she lived here during the rebellion against the bandits.'

送下了说哩，陀的阿大陀啊送下了去了。
sũ=xɤ=lɔ   u   li,   tha=tɤ   ata   tha   sũ=xɤ=lɔ   tɕhi=lɔ.
give=COMP=PFV say PART LRP=GEN father LRP:ACC give=COMP=PFV go=PFV

'Her father sent her here and left.'

去了着陀仗打罢了来说着，
tɕhi=lɔ=tʂɤ   tha   tʂã   ta=pa=lɔ   lɛ   u=tʂɤ,
go=PFV=PROG   LRP   battle   fight=finish=PFV come   say=PROG

'He said he was going to war and would come back after the war.'

嘚来没来，撂下了说哩。
tɤ   lɛ   mi   lɛ,   liɔ=xɤ=lɔ   u   li.
DM   come   NEG   come   throw=COMP=PFV   say   PART

'Later he did not come back and left her here.'

撂下了嘚一阵，
liɔ=xɤ=lɔ   tɤ   itʂɤ̃,
throw=COMP=PFV   DM   period_of_time
丢下了有一段时间，

三十晚夕我的阿奶他馍馍要去了说哩。
sãʂiuãɕi   ŋɤ=tɤ   anɛ   tha   mɤmɤ   iɔ   tɕhi=lɔ
new_year's_eve   1=GEN   grandmother   LRP   steamed_bread   beg   go=PFV
u   li.
say   PART

'After living here for a while, on New Year's Eve, my grandmother went to ask for steamed bread to eat.'

这么说着个，经常我们啊话攀着个呀。
tʂɤmɤ   ʂuɤ=tʂɤ   kɤ,   tɕĩtʂhã   ŋɤ=ma   xua   phã=tɤ   kɤ   ia.
this_way say=PROG PART often   1=PL:DAT   words chat=PROG PART PART
'That's how often she talked to us (about these past events).'

II. List of abbreviations

1	first-person
2	second-person
3	third-person
ABL	ablative
ACC	accusative
CM	comparative
COM	comitative
COMP	complement verb/marker
COND	conditional
CONJ	conjunctive coordinator
DAT	dative
DISJ	disjunctive coordinator
DISP	disposal
DM	discourse marker
EXP	experiential
FUT	future
GEN	genitive
ING	ingressive
INS	instrumental
LOC	locative
LRP	locutor-referential pronoun
NEG	negative
NOMZ	nominalizer
ORD	ordinary
PART	particle
PFV	perfective
PL	plural
PN	proper name
POST	postposition
PROHIBIT	prohibitive
Q	question marker
REL	relativizer
RES	resultative

TAG   tag question
VIM   valence-increasing marker

Notes

1 Literally, 洋 *iã* means foreign. In the old days, many products were imported from other countries.
2 Ma Bufang 马步芳 (1903–1975) was a warlord in the Gansu and Qinghai Provinces during the Republic of China era. To the common people of Zhoutun, he was a sort of bandit who brought wars.

Index

Note: Page locators in **bold** indicate a table.

addressee 23, 30, 112
adjective: identifying 2, 15, 17, 59; intensifying/enhancing 60–1; as modifiers 15, 62–3; phrase 46, 111; as predicates 60, 63; reduplicated 68; typical 63
adpositions: postposition (tɕhiã 前) 107–8; preposition (uã 往) 105–7
adverb: common 66–8; expression 43; positioning 64–5; reduplication 17, 68
adverbial (modifies/defines a verb) 17, 71, 109
adverbial clause 136–7
Aikhenvald, Alexandra 5, 47, 49, 64
Amdo Tibetan 1, 3–5, 45, 112, 119
animate referent 23, 77–8
ARTV (agent, recipient, theme, verb) 2, 118

bare noun 29, 79
bare predicate 64
benefactive (meaning) 23, 53, 55
Bhat, Darbhe N. Shankara 38

Chinese: dialect 50, 57, 70, 106
classifiers: nominal 87; verbal 88–90
clause structure: basic word order 116–18; copula structure 119–20; ditransitive construction 118–19; OV/VO order 116–17
comparative clause: comparative construction 122–6

constructions: comparative 64, 122, 124–5
coordinators: conjunctive (tɛ 带) 109; disjunctive (不是 puʂi and 么 mʏ) 110–15
copula structure 119–20

dative-accusative: enclitic 69–70; marker 13; syncretism 22, 24
demonstratives: manner/degree (这么 tʂʏmʏ and 那么 namʏ) 81
demonstratives: animate/inanimate referents 77–9; location referents (kʏ and kuʏ) 79–80; system (proximal 个 kʏ and distal 箇 kuʏ) 77
ditransitive construction 2, 70, 118–19
Dixon, Robert M.W. 5

experiencer (conveys subjective feelings) 23–4, 79

final particles: amalgamated (ta 哒) 98; background information (sa 撒) 102–4; common 90, **104**, 135; declarative (ti 嘀) 90–2; final position (xuã 喤) 95–6; imperative (ia 呀) 99–100; interrogative (pa 吧) 92–3; multi-functional (li 哩) 93–5; neutral (kʏ 个) 96–8; obvious (pi 呗) 101; question (mʏ) 100; speculation/deduction 41–2

Gan-Qing linguistic area 4–5, 116

Han people 3

interrogative: clauses *(tɕi)* (X) 131–2; pronouns 16, 26; sentences 90, 92, 96, 103
interrogative clause: alternative questions 132; tag questions 132–3; Wh-questions 131–2; yes-no questions 131
interrogative words: -mɤ *words* 83–4; a-*words* 82–3; atypical (几 *tɕi* and 来 *lɛ*) 84–6; tuɤ-*words* 81–2
intonation **104**, 120, 130–1

Li, Charles N. 137
linguistic identity 2, 4–5
linguistic inventory typology (LIT) 5
Liu, Danqing 5, 39, 125

Mandarin Chinese: classifiers 87; disposal marker 106; influence of 1, 3, 5–6; phonology 10, 33, 37; word patterns 69, 72; word phrases 18, 55
markers: ablative (=tha) 22, 26; accusative (=xa/a) 24, 70, 73, 100; aspect (了 =lɔ, 着 =tʂɤ 过 =kuɤ) 29, 32, 34, 38, 97, 135; attributive (的 *tɤ*) 62; comitative-instrumental (=lã) 22, 24–5; comparative (看 *khã*) 22, 29, 122; conditional *(ɕi)* 114; dative *(=xa)* 22–4, 28, 58, 79, 118; genitive (=tɤ) 28, 70, 117, 134–5; locative (=li and =xã) 26, 28, 80, 105, 120; negative *(pu)* (不 *pu*) 39, 65; passive 57; perfective *(=lɔ)* 33–4, 37–8, 91, 135; postpositional 1, 22, 136; productive (*ti*-第) 16; prohibitive (要 *pɔ*) 61, 130; question (么 *mɤ*) 131; resultative (=pa) 37
Mongolic language 4–5
Monguor/Tu people 3
monosyllabic: adjective 62–3, 68; morpheme (phonemic tones) 11, 15; nominal classifiers 87; noun 62

negative copula 45, 112
nominalizer 16, 45
Northwest Chinese 2, 71, 106
noun: case relation 22; compounding 18–19; construction 15;
demonstrative 15, 79; function 14, 16–17, 26, 30–1; generic noun 29; phrases 45, 107, 110, 114; reduplication 17–18; referentiality 29–31; word formation 15–17
numerals: cardinal/ordinal 86; fractional 86; phrase (+classifier) 31, 86, 88; placement 15–16, 88–9

OV (object-verb) 2, 5, 105, 116–18, 135

possessor 23, 58
predicate: as adjective 63; compounding 18; constructions 119, 125–6; expression (induces subject feelings) 23, 59–60; word order (copula) 116
pronoun: first person 69, 73, 128; locator-referential (LRP) 71–6, 155–6; reflexive 19, 71; second person 70, 107, 112, 128; third person 70–3

Qiaohua (dialect) 3, 71
Qinghai Province, China 1

recipient 2, 23, 55, 70, 118
referentiality: defined as 29; generic 29–30; individual 30–1

Sandman, Erika 1
single marker: placement 15–16
Sinitic language 1–2, 4–5, 10
SOV (subject-object-verb) word order 1–2, 18, 112, 116, 135
subjective feelings 23–4
subordinate clause: adverbial clause 136–7; compliment clause 135; relative clause 134–5
syntactic distribution 59, 120–1

Thompson, Sandra 137
three-dimensional space 26–7
Tibetan people 3–4
tone: lexical 2 (*see also* word tones); phonemic 2, 10–11
tone numbers 11
topic structure 137–8

Turkic language 4–5
typological features 2, 24

verbs: complement constructions 49–52; degree constructions 52–3; deontic modality 42–4; dynamic modality 39–41; evidentiality 44–5; epistemic modality 41–2; experiential *(=kuʳ)* 38; expression of tense 38; features of 32; future aspect (哩 =*li*) 34–5; ingressive (脱 =*thuʳ* and 开 =*khɛ*) 35–6; negation 45–6; perfective *(=lɔ)* 33–4; possession and existence 58; progressive (着 =*tʂʳ*) 36–7; result constructions 52; resultative (罢 =*pa*) 37; serial verb constructions (SVC) 46–9; valance changing 53–7; verbal classifier 88
VO (verb-object) 5, 105, 116

word tones 2, 10–12, 18
Wutun 1

Xu, Dan 5
Xu, Qiulan 3

Zhang, Bojiang 63
Zhe, Wankui 4
Zhou, Chenlei 90, 115
Zhou, Jian 4, 113
Zhoutun: tonal system 2; village 3–4, 50

For Product Safety Concerns and Information please contact our EU representative GPSR@taylorandfrancis.com
Taylor & Francis Verlag GmbH, Kaufingerstraße 24, 80331 München, Germany

www.ingramcontent.com/pod-product-compliance
Lightning Source LLC
Chambersburg PA
CBHW051746230426
43670CB00012B/2182